In Spite of All the Devils

In Spite of All the Devils

Linda Hope

Tampa, Florida

This book is a work of fiction. The names, characters and events in this book are the products of the author's imagination or are used fictitiously. Any similarity to real persons living or dead is coincidental and not intended by the author.

The content associated with this book is the sole work and responsibility of the author. Gatekeeper Press had no involvement in the generation of this content.

In Spite of All the Devils

Published by Gatekeeper Press
7853 Gunn Hwy., Suite 209
Tampa, FL 33626
www.GatekeeperPress.com

Copyright © 2024 by Linda Hope
All rights reserved. Neither this book, nor any parts within it may be sold or reproduced in any form or by any electronic or mechanical means, including information storage and retrieval systems, without permission in writing from the author. The only exception is by a reviewer, who may quote short excerpts in a review.

The cover design, interior formatting, typesetting, and editorial work for this book are entirely the product of the author. Gatekeeper Press did not participate in and is not responsible for any aspect of these elements.

Library of Congress Control Number: 2024914800

ISBN (hardcover): 9781662957086
ISBN (paperback): 9781662957093
eISBN: 9781662957109

Image "Bombed, Building" by tookapic from Pixabay.
"Girl, Child, Portrait" image by aamiraimer from Pixabay.

For First-Time Readers

For those who are reading my book for the first time, I would like to provide some information. I understand it is very important to let you know how I chose my pen name.

Linda

I chose the name *Linda* because a woman named Linda introduced my father, Vladimir, to my mother, Maria. Linda is my father's sister. This is very important to me. If Linda hadn't helped my dad meet my mom, you wouldn't be reading this book, and I wouldn't exist in our land. Thank you so much, Linda. I'll never forget you.

Hope

I took the surname *Hope* for two reasons. The first very important reason is that I have a granddaughter named Arabella Hope. She is a first-generation American. I love her so much.

The second reason is that I have been living all my life hoping for something good to happen to me. Hope is what I put into just about everything in my life. Hope for every day, for every occasion—that's what gave me the strength to survive and live. I achieved so much in my life just because I did not lose my *hope* for survival, for life, for happiness, for all that I have had and will have every day.

So the combination of these two strong words gave me the strength to be the author Linda Hope.

These two names gave me hope in myself.

Thank you, Linda and Hope!

Advice from the Author

Do you have a low spirit? Do not lose heart. I will give you some advice: do not lower your head and do not lose hope. Get angry at that which tries to suppress you. Raise your head; look at the cloudless deep blue sky. Look into the depths of His never-ending hope. Somewhere out there is your dream. Achieve what you dream of and do not give up in any situation. *Survive on the evil of all the devils.*

I will tell you a story of when I lived in an orphanage where thirty girls—or maybe more—who had no parents lived. Each of the girls had their own dreams, but not all of them were achieved.

I was only nine years old. From the window of my bedroom, every morning, I looked out at the cloudless deep blue sky, and I dreamed of turning into a little bird, breaking out of this cage to freedom. That was what I got out of bed for—the fact that, one day, I would break out of that cage and would have to be ready to live in that other world. I had to be ready for it. That was why I began to read a lot. I read everything that came my way.

One day, I broke free. I was glad that I had survived and that I was now a free-flying bird. But I did not know that, without experience and guidance from parents, it is very difficult to get used to this new world.

I made mistake after mistake, and they were what made me a strong person. I am proud of myself for having gone through many unpredictable situations in my life. I nevertheless gradually achieved success. I never lost my hope, and whenever I had a very difficult situation in my life, I investigated the deep heavens. It was these moments that gave me deep hope and strength. I battled in an orphanage. I survived my teenage years. I survived in Russia. I understood and learned a lot. I could not understand the behavior of people living in Russia. I didn't agree with a lot. That's why I went to America. I wanted to be free. I wanted to have my own opinion. I wanted to make my own decision without pressure from anyone. I am proud that I have become such a person.

My advice is don't lose your dream but pursue it, no matter what the cost. Because, believe me, no one will ever stand in your way if they see that you have fortitude, perseverance, and faith in yourself. It is very important to believe in yourself–and only in yourself. Listen to all possible advice but make your own decisions, including forming your own opinions. Most importantly, never lose your hope. Cherish this strong feeling forever. Hope is not only a word, but it is also the strength of your spirit, and you will need it throughout your life.

About the Book

The Russian forces' devastation of Mariupol and continued efforts to erase Ukrainian culture stand out as one of the worst chapters of their large-scale invasion of Ukraine.

I decided to call this book *In Spite of All the Devils* because the girl who is the main character of this book found the strength to overcome all kinds of difficulties. And having overcome them despite everything, she was able to start her life in a new country. She proved to be so strong in character that she survived and was still able to help her younger brother, to become strong, to not give up in the face of anything, not difficulties, tragic moments in her life, the struggle for survival, or even death.

This book is about a close friend from my youth. The war has caused difficulties, and I'm proud of her and her family for their heroic courage and devotion to the Motherland. We need to have such people in our land. I'm sure that everyone will agree with me.

I stand with my head bowed before you, my friends, before your children and your friends, who are fighting for a happy future for our children and grandchildren.

Chapter 1
Martha

A blonde girl was sitting on a bench on the grounds of the Lviv Medical University–one of the oldest and biggest medical universities in Ukraine.

Her name was Martha. That year, she was finishing her studies. She was ready to start her responsible work. She had gotten an education, and now she could work. Registered nurses were registered and licensed by each state to care for patients. Some nurses focused on a certain field, such as surgery. Operating room nurses were certified in various areas of surgery. Nurses had to pass an exam to be certified as a nurse in the surgical department.

With only a few days left before she would receive her diploma, she felt a sense of joy and pride that she would be helping the surgeon in the operating room during operations. She knew that her education did not end there. She would study to be a surgeon, but she had decided that she needed to gain experience observing what was happening on the operating table first.

She said, "I want to get logical thinking and correct decision-making, in any case. The patient's life depends on making the right decision."

Martha had just turned twenty-one. She was tall and thin and had wavy hair. No matter how she styled it, you would think she had just come out of the beauty salon. She had huge bright green eyes, and her black eyebrows gave her face a confident character. She was an intelligent girl. Her lips seemed like they were drawn on her face with a bright-red pencil. These words were uttered by all her friends when describing her lips.

Martha was a very beautiful girl, and this always upset her. She wanted to look normal; she didn't want to stand out. But you couldn't argue with a gift of nature. That was why she was not friends with any of the men. All the young men who would like to date her looked like actors in the movies, and she wanted to meet a man without particularly attractive facial features.

And it was for this reason that she sat on the bench alone. The young men whom she refused to meet were offended by her, and the young men who wanted to date her were afraid to meet her, as they were afraid that she would refuse them.

Martha just sat on a bench and admired the students around her. Some just sat on the grass and were glad that they had finally finished their studies. By their behavior, one could understand that they were ready to accept their diplomas and to take a solemn oath which would always haunt them throughout their lives—being responsible health care workers.

The next day, a ceremony was held to issue their diplomas. Martha felt happy. For some reason, her heart beat faster than usual. Well, her mood was elated; now she felt like a necessary person for society. She always took great responsibility in handling everything. And it was this feeling that had led her to the field of medicine.

After receiving her diploma, she immediately went home. She wanted to share her joy with her relatives. Always surrounded by her parents, she had received a great upbringing. Her parents taught her to be responsible and keep her promises. She grew up to be a strong, unshakable person. It was her parents who molded her to become very strong in character.

She was born and raised in Mariupol, in the Donbass region. She loved her city and missed it. It had been five years since she had lived there, and whenever she came to visit her parents on vacation, she met her classmates and friends whom she had known over the years. It always brought her great pleasure to meet her old friends from her childhood and adolescence.

Mariupol was a beautiful, modern city. The school where she had spent ten years of her childhood and adolescence was located near her home. It had been very convenient for her because it took practically no time to get to school. She had enjoyed a walk in the morning when she went to school. Martha had always went alone, but after school, she would usually return home with a group of her classmates and students who lived in the neighborhood.

When she came home after graduating from university, she felt that the city looked different somehow. There were constant demonstrations against the Ukrainian government and, of course, retaliatory demonstrations against the invasion and interference of the Russian government.

This began to happen after Ukraine separated from Russia. Ukraine had become an independent state. It embarked on a democratic path of development.

Martha had decided she would be aware of all the affairs but would not interfere. She would not take part in demonstrations, not in Ukraine, not in Russia.

Her mother had been born in and graduated from school in Russia. After graduating from school, she had come to Mariupol, where she met a boy who was born there. He was now considered Ukrainian, and she was considered Russian. They had a daughter, Martha, and a son, Viktor.

According to many Russians, Martha's mother should fight on the side of the Russian population against the Ukrainians, so against her husband and her children. What nonsense and indescribable stupidity.

After graduating from the university, the Lviv Regional Hospital invited Martha to work there. Of course, she accepted this invitation. After spending only two weeks at home with her family, she returned to Lviv.

The political situation in Mariupol worried her very much. But she decided to focus on her work. This was the way of life. She chose to help people and not turn them against each other. She rented an apartment in Lviv near her job, and again, she didn't need much time to get to work.

She thought, *I am always lucky for the location of my work and my home. And as a child, for the location of my school and my home.* At this thought, for some reason, a smile appeared on Martha's face. Such a small detail in her life brought her pleasure.

On the first day of her work, she met a surgeon named Josef. She was to work on all the surgeries performed by his group.

Josef was tall, with a sturdy build, and he somewhat resembled her father, Ivan, very kind but strict. He told Martha his requirements for the operation. He was very focused; everything was organized flawlessly. But after the operation, he told funny stories and anecdotes.

In normal life, he was the center of attention. It was very easy and pleasant to be around him, but in the operating room, he turned into a strict and incomparably serious person. Some called him "the robot"–behind his back, of course.

Martha thought, *I don't see anything wrong with this. Josef is a surgeon, and he has a huge responsibility on his shoulders.*

Martha very quickly joined the team. Everyone respected her. She somehow reminded them of Josef . . . very serious and responsible at work and funny and warm-hearted in real life.

Chapter 2
Broken Heart

Two years flew by very quickly. Martha fell in love with the city of Lviv. She made new friends and acquaintances. She became used to her work and took it very seriously. She was always reminded of the days she had spent at her parents' house after university. She was worried about her parents because of the political views in Ukraine.

Martha realized that the situation was becoming increasingly tense between the Ukrainian and Russian populations.

One evening, she called her parents. Her mom answered the call.

"Good evening," Martha said. Her first question was "Well, how is your political situation?"

Her mom, of course, did not want to upset her. She replied, "We're fine."

Martha did not believe her. "I see what is shown on TV, and I hear what they say on the radio. Tell the truth; what's going on there?" asked Martha in a demanding and insistent voice.

"I am telling you the truth," replied Maria, her mother. "We just don't interfere in these matters. And no one is bothering us about it."

"But that doesn't change the tense political state in the city," replied Martha.

After a long conversation, she offered to share her home in Lviv with her parents, but they would not agree to move.

Her father kept saying, "I hope and believe in people. One day, they will all understand that this is all just a delusion, that there is no difference between Ukrainians and Russians. We are all just people, fathers, mothers, and children."

But Martha's premonition did not let her down.

Martha was in the operating room while all the other workers were watching the TV. Russia was bombing the city of Mariupol.

The bombing erased this beautiful, historical city from the face of the earth. Mariupol was practically destroyed; all buildings were razed to the ground.

Martha did not yet know that one of the bombs had hit her parents' house, the house where she and her brother, Viktor, had been born and raised. When Martha was young, she had considered her home a refuge from everything that happened to her. Whatever happened to her, she had known that, when she came home, her family and parents would calm her down and protect her from everything that was happening. That home, which was kept in her heart, had been the strongest fortress throughout her childhood and adolescent years.

When the operation was over, everyone left the operating room, and Martha continued to talk to Josef about the ongoing operation. They were on their way to the waiting room when, suddenly, Martha noticed the TV that was in the room.

Josef approached a woman who was expecting the results of her husband's ongoing surgery. He explained that everything had gone well and that she would be able to visit him tomorrow.

After finishing the conversation, he turned and saw Martha looking at the TV, her face whiter than the hospital wall.

Josef walked up to her, took her hand, and said, "Come to my office. We'll call your parents right away."

Martha did not hear a single word that Josef had said to her. Everyone looked at Martha; they all knew that her parents lived in Mariupol.

Josef took her hand, pulled her into the office, and sat her down in a chair.

Martha did not cry. She was shocked. Josef dialed the phone number of her parents. It was written down in his notebook. He had to know the phone numbers of all relatives of all the employees who worked with him.

The telephone call was immediately interrupted. There was no signal.

The war has begun, he thought. *The Russian government has gone mad.* It was all spinning in his head.

He dialed the phone number that belonged to Martha's parents again, and again, there was no reaction. There was no busy signal, just silence, as if this number belonged to another planet.

He looked at Martha, and she looked at him in silence.

Suddenly, she said, "I have to go home. I have to go home." She kept repeating it.

Martha had realized that she had to leave for Mariupol as soon as possible. She had to find her parents and get them out of the war zone. She looked at Josef and said, "I'm sorry, but I have to go to Mariupol now."

"Yes," he replied. "I agree with you. Don't get upset about your work. We'll all be waiting for you. And we will pray that your parents are alive and well. There is just no connection," he reassured Martha.

"Let's hope so," she replied.

Martha had never known that she had a huge amount of willpower inside and that her character was capable of handling any difficult circumstances.

She was very quick to get home. She collected the essentials for her trip. She decided that she would get to her home faster if she drove her car. Martha tried to call again, but there was no change in communication. There was simply no connection.

After leaving, she tried to drive quickly while carefully observing all the traffic rules. For some reason, there were almost no cars on the road. Then, she noticed that all the cars were going in the opposite direction.

Oh my gosh, she thought. *Everyone is fleeing from the war zone.* Like lightning, the words flew through her mind.

"Yes," she said. "This is war. Russia has decided to conquer the territory of Ukraine. Russia does not recognize a free Ukraine."

Then, she thought, *Now I know on which side I will speak. Russia destroyed the city where I grew up. Only because we are now considered a free, democratic Ukraine.*

She drove alone the whole way. Sometimes, there were military vehicles with soldiers. On the way, she came across one car parked in the middle of the road, as if blocking the way to Mariupol.

A soldier approached her and said, "I'd like to know where you're going."

"I'm going to Mariupol," Martha replied.

The soldier began to explain to her that it would be better if she went back. "I hope you understand that this is very dangerous. Mariupol is currently under fire from the Russian side. It is very dangerous to be in the Mariupol area," he tried to explain to Martha.

But Martha answered briefly and surely, "I will go to Mariupol. My parents are there. I have to pick them up. And I'm a nurse; maybe I can help the victims."

She was afraid that she might not be allowed to pass, which was why she had added that she was a nurse. The second half of her sentence played a huge role.

"A nurse? Then we will be happy to accompany you," said the soldier.

"Thank you," Martha replied.

The soldiers returned to the car, and they followed her for quite a long time, almost all the way to Mariupol.

"Thank you," Martha said, approaching the driver after they arrived at Mariupol. "Now I will go to the area of my house. Tell me your address, then I will stop by and try to help you as much as I can afterwards."

Martha drove slowly because the roads were full of huge holes. In some places, it was very difficult to determine where the road was because it was almost destroyed. The houses around the road were destroyed, as if they'd never been there.

Driving into her street—if this place could be called a street, since it was impossible to understand where the road was and where the houses were—she saw a group of soldiers with dogs.

A group of rescuers, thought Martha.

Martha stopped, or rather, they stopped her. One of the team members approached the car. He said, "It is very dangerous to travel in this place. What are you doing here?"

Martha opened the doors and got out of the car. She did not see the soldiers. She looked in the direction where her house had once stood. Only ruins remained of the house. She ran screaming in the direction of her house, but the soldiers stopped her.

"No, no!" shouted one. "Hold her."

Two soldiers held Martha, but she struggled to escape.

The man who stopped her approached her, realizing that this was her home. "Do you live here?" he asked.

"Yes, my parents are there. You have to help them. My parents are there." And then she cried out, "Mother! Father! Where are you? This is Martha, I'm here, I'll help you now."

The two soldiers were still holding her.

"I am a nurse. I have to examine them. Where are my parents?" shouted Martha, and then she noticed that, on the ground near the destroyed house, there were two stretchers. They were both covered with white sheets.

Suddenly, Martha realized the horror of what had happened. She immediately fell silent.

She looked at one of the soldiers and asked, "Are these my parents?"

"We don't know. It's very difficult to identify them." Then, he asked, "Can you do that?"

Martha said, "Yes, I have to see them."

A man in a white coat approached. It was clear that he was a doctor. He said, "Did I hear you're a nurse?"

"Yes," replied Martha.

"Fine," he replied. "We need your help. We found a young man, and he is unconscious, but his leg is injured. Can you help us?"

"Yes," replied Martha.

They went toward the car where the patient was. Martha recognized him at once.

"This is my brother," she said. Martha examined the patient and applied everything necessary to his injured leg.

Martha behaved heroically. She pulled herself together, and she did everything necessary that she could do as a nurse.

After providing help to her brother, she asked the doctor, "And now I want to examine these two bodies. Do I have to verify that they are my parents or not?" There was a small hope in her soul that these were not her parents.

The doctor said, "Come on." He made it clear to the two soldiers to follow them.

Approaching the stretchers, Martha squatted down.

The doctor asked, "Are you ready?"

Martha couldn't answer; she just nodded her head. In her soul, there was hope that these were not her parents, but at the same time, she was afraid of the horror that she would see.

The doctor slowly opened one of the sheets on the stretchers. Martha was horrified by what she saw. She worked in a hospital, but it was something she had not seen in all her work. The body was damaged by the explosion, from the impact of the surrounding walls, from the fire—all this was done to the body, which was in a completely unrecognizable state.

Martha wasn't sure if it was her dad or her mom.

She said, "Let's see the second body."

She said "the body." She didn't want to say her father; she didn't want to say her mom. She was still hoping for a miracle.

But unfortunately, they were her parents. The soldiers had pulled them out of the rubble and the remains of the house where Martha had once lived.

The doctor opened the second sheet, and Martha immediately recognized her mother. She had a ring on her right hand which her husband had given her on their fiftieth anniversary of marriage.

Martha sat down on the ground and put the palms of her hands on her face with such force that it seemed pain had pierced her heart. She sobbed so loudly that everyone paid attention to her. Martha knelt and wanted to hug her mother's body. But she was kept from doing so. Her mother's face was not damaged. Martha could not take her eyes away from her. She did not want to believe that her parents had died so cruelly and without any valid reason.

Maria, Martha's mother, had been born in Russia and only after graduating from college had she stayed and lived in Mariupol. A Russian woman, mother, and wife had been killed by Russian soldiers under the leadership of the Russian government.

Does a human life mean absolutely nothing?

A Russian mother of two children had been killed only because she had chosen to live in Mariupol. She had been killed only because the Russian government had decided that they needed to return the territory of Ukraine to Russia.

A small plot of land was much more precious than a human life for the leaders of Russia.

It did not matter to them at all that someone would lose their mother, father, brother, or sister. It was important to them that the plot of land where they lived came under the influence of Russia.

After the conquest of this area, new families would come there, also Russian, without thinking about the fact that someone had died there, the same people, just like them. How scary it was that some people did not have a sense of responsibility for their terrible actions.

How do such people sleep at night? Without guilt? Martha thought. *I do not consider such people to be people. They are beasts who don't understand the guilt, resentment, and pain endured by innocent people.*

Several soldiers approached Martha, took her by the arms, and led her to the car.

The doctor gave her a sedative and said, "I won't let you drive your car like that. We are now going to a mobile hospital. There we will agree on everything."

Those were the last words that Martha heard.

The medicine took over her, and Martha fell sound asleep. The doctor had done what he had to. He had given her a double dose to make her fall asleep. Martha had been under an enormous amount of stress.

She woke up in a large ward, surrounded by injured soldiers and wounded people. She looked around, and only one thought came to her mind: *They are lucky they survived.*

She tried to sit on the bed, but the dose of sedative medicine was so big that she didn't have the strength to sit up.

A nurse came up to her. "Hello, Martha," she said. "My name is Irina. I am also a nurse, like you. The doctor told me about your situation. How do you feel?" she asked.

Martha asked, "Did you give me a double dose of sedative?"

"Yes, a little more. You needed it. You were very shocked by what happened," replied Irina.

"How long have I slept?" asked Martha.

"I don't know," replied Irina. She deceived Martha; she just didn't want to tell her.

Martha needed rest as long as possible. She really had been in shock. Her blood pressure had jumped, and her heart had been beating at 140 beats per minute. The doctor had taken all possible measures to calm her down.

Irina said, "It's late. I suggest you sleep one more night with us, and tomorrow, we'll arrange everything for you."

Irina did not go into details, but she wrapped Martha more comfortably. She gave her a glass of water with sleeping pills and placed several glasses of water next to her.

A new group of wounded soldiers was brought to the hospital. There was a lot of work to be done. Irina was glad when Martha fell asleep. She needed to calm down and return to a normal physical state since she had to take the car all the way to Lviv. The city was located on the opposite side of Ukraine, almost on the border of Poland and Germany.

The next morning, Martha woke up and felt like a normal person physically. She was ready for her journey from Mariupol to Lviv. *The last trip with my parents*, she thought, and she cried again.

She found the doctor she had met near her destroyed house. His name was Leo.

When he saw her, he said, "Martha, I decided to help you. It will be much easier for you to transfer your parents in an urn instead of in a coffin, so we did your parents' cremation. I hope you remember that we talked about it."

"Yes, I gave you this idea. Thank you," she replied. "Where's my brother?"

"He's ready to go; I've just talked to him," Leo replied. "Let's go," he suggested, and they went to another room.

Approaching Viktor, Martha was glad to see that he looked completely different. He was physically almost healthy; only one leg had a fracture.

Martha did not ask him questions. She thought, *He will tell me himself when we're on the road to Lviv.*

Leo said, "The soldiers will help your brother get to the car, and we'll go get your parents' urns." He gazed at Martha, as if asking her, "Are you ready for this?"

Martha looked back at him, tears streaming down her cheeks.

Leo took her hand. "Remember how we were taught in medical school to be strong, to be patient, and to feel like we were helping someone who needed our help?" asked Leo. "That's what you're doing now. You're taking your brother and your parents to your home. And there's nothing you can do to change what happened. Your job now is to step forward and do what you're supposed to do, for them. And most importantly, now you must think about yourself. They have nobody else but you, and you must be strong for them first. You have a heavy responsibility ahead of you, to help your brother recover and to find a place to bury your parents. Do you think you're up to the task? Or do you need my help?"

Martha stared at him all this time, not blinking. *What a strong and responsible person*, she thought.

He asked again, "Martha, can you hear me?"

Martha perked up. "Yes, I hear you. Don't worry, I can handle it. My mother said that I am very strong in character, and in any situation, I always help others. That's why I went to study medicine. My plans included studying to be a surgeon. I don't know how I'm going to do it now because it's war. But I'm sure it will come to fruition somehow. I'm sure of it," she replied.

Leo looked at her and thought, *What an unshakable spirit and strong character for such a young girl. What a pity that she lives so far away.* Catching himself in this thought, he smiled slightly, turning away.

They entered a nearby building and drew up all the documents very quickly. A woman came out of the other room, two cardboard boxes in hand. Martha was surprised. They were not urns but boxes.

The woman explained, "I'm sorry, but we don't have urns. We give out boxes. They have the day of death and the name. We don't know the exact time. It will be very easy for you to transfer them into the urns."

Martha came up to her and took the boxes, pressed her hands to her chest, and cried again. Holding both boxes near her chest, she walked out of the building.

Leo followed her in silence. He did not want to interrupt her thoughts. He knew what she was thinking now, and it was very difficult for him to help her in any way. He also felt her pain. He had lost his parents in a car accident when he was only twenty-five years old. He was aware of what was going on in Martha's soul now.

They silently continued to walk to the car where Viktor was sitting. Martha put the boxes on her brother's lap and said,

"Once upon a time, you sat on Dad and Mom's laps, and now, they will sit on your lap and at home."

"With great pleasure," he replied, and he put one hand on the box where his mother's ashes were and his second hand on the box where his father's ashes were.

Martha turned to the doctor, thanking him for everything. She looked at him, and he looked into her eyes, and they both wept in silence. Martha embraced him and laid her head on his shoulder. She felt his warmth and regret for what had happened. At this moment, she thought that she had met an extraordinary person.

Leo and Martha had some kind of understanding, without any explanation.

"I am very glad that you are going to Lviv, away from here. I think that the war will not reach Lviv," he said. "And if it does, we'll meet again."

"I know where you work," she said.

And then, suddenly, he asked, "Martha, can I call you?"

Martha replied, "I'll call you when we get home." And then she realized with embarrassment that she liked him. She added, "I'll tell you how we got there."

"Yes, of course. I'll be very happy," he replied.

They looked into each other's eyes again, and neither of them wanted to part, and neither of them said goodbye.

Finally, Martha came to her senses. "Thank you for everything. I don't know how I would have survived all this without you," she said. "Thank you."

"See you soon," Leo said.

"See you soon," replied Martha.

Neither of them understand why they had said, "See you soon." They both understood that the war wouldn't end in Mariupol.

CHAPTER 3

Scary Details

When Martha left the city of Mariupol, she was silent. Her brother, Viktor, said, "I don't want to tell you about everything that happened now since you're driving."

Martha replied confidently, "Tell me. I want to know. I can't live in guessing anymore."

"Are you sure about that?" asked Viktor.

"Yes, I'm sure of it," Martha replied.

"Okay," Viktor agreed. "Mom cooked dinner, and it turned out that we had no bread, so Mom said, 'Viktor, please run to get bread. We don't have bread. What do you think, we should go get them to buy it? Or will we eat without bread?' Dad and I were watching TV. Dad said, 'I would like to have bread,' and looked at me. I understood him without explanation. I went outside, and as soon as I opened the gate doors, I heard some strange sound. I raised my head up, and then I felt myself fly up into the air, and after that, I don't remember anything.

"Mom saved my life. She sent me to buy bread. If I'd stayed with Dad and watched TV, I would have been killed by that bomb too. Now tell me what you saw when you arrived. Did you find Dad and Mom in the house?" he asked.

"No," replied Martha. "I arrived after the soldiers had already found our father and mother. I saw a couple of stretchers, and they were lying on them. The doctor did not allow me to enter the house, or rather, the remains of our house. There's nothing left there. Just a mountain of ruined remnants.

"The most difficult thing for me was to identify the bodies of our father and mother. It was very difficult to recognize Dad, and only when I recognized our mother did I realize that it was our dad. They also told me about you. I put a splint on your leg, and you were taken to the hospital. They gave me a sedative. I slept for a long time; I don't know how long. They cremated our parents so it's easier to move them from one place to another. You know the rest."

Viktor read "Maria" on the box. He picked up the box, hugged her, and said, "Thank you, Mom, for saving my life." Viktor added, "I think she knew she had to send me somewhere away from home. She had a premonition to save me from something very scary. She never asked me to buy bread in the evening. And we didn't need bread. She was cooking cutlets and buckwheat."

Martha said, "Viktor, you know that Dad eats everything with bread, even bread with bread," she said, smiling, pleasant memories flashing through her head.

"Mom asked me when she was cooking a patty, 'Viktor, what kind of cutlets would you like for dinner?' I replied, 'Mom, make them with an egg inside. They are very tasty with buckwheat.' She cooked exactly what I asked for. The smell was so good. I even now remember that smell."

"Interesting," said Martha. "Mom made you the last dinner. Unfortunately, you didn't have time to try those cutlets. Well, you're going to remember that for the rest of your life."

Viktor said, "Thank you, Mom, for my delicious dinner. It wasn't the last. I will remember you every time I eat cutlets with buckwheat."

They remembered their parents throughout their journey from Mariupol to Lviv.

When they got home, they were both very tired and depressed from everything that had happened in Mariupol and everything that had happened during the journey.

Martha said, "I'll cook dinner—your buckwheat patties—and we'll remember Mom and Dad, and I have a surprise for you."

"What kind of surprise?" asked Viktor. "I do not like any surprises for now."

"You will like this one," answered Martha.

They were both in the kitchen while Martha cooked. She set the table and helped Viktor sit down. The table was set for four.

"This is for me, this is for you, this is for Dad, and this is for Mom," Martha explained. She poured four glasses of wine. "Our dinner, together with the whole family, as before. Every year, like today, we will have a family dinner. We will be together, and today, Dad and Mom will give us their rings."

Martha took two rings from her pocket, one from her father's hand and the other from her mother's. "This is for you, Viktor, from Dad," she said and handed him the ring.

Viktor took it, kissed it, and put it on his left hand. "I'll put it on my right hand when I get married," he added.

Martha took the ring from her mother and did the same. The ring was the perfect size; it sat on her finger very beautifully. Their father had given this ring to their mother for the fiftieth anniversary of their marriage. The ring held a very beautiful red ruby, and around it was an openwork weave of gold, a very original ring. Their father had ordered it especially for that day. By his order and by his drawing.

Maria had loved this ring from the first moment she'd seen it, and as soon as she saw it, her mother had said, "This ring will be yours when I move to Heaven."

Martha had said, "Mom, I'll be happy if you wear this ring for another fifty years."

Her mother had laughed.

Martha remembered very well that day, that moment. Maria had been so happy and joyful. It had been a beautiful evening, with friends and close relatives invited.

"Yes," said Viktor. "What a pity that she wore this ring for only one year."

"Fate," said Martha. "You can't argue with it."

"Fate?" asked Viktor. "No, this is not fate. This is the hatred of the Russian government for Ukraine. As soon as I recover, I will immediately go to the army and fight for our independence."

Martha was frightened by these words; she did not want to lose her brother.

That was all she had left in the present time, only one brother. She decided that, as soon as he recovered, she would get him a job in her hospital and monitor his actions.

The next day, she went to work. Everyone there already knew what had happened since Leo had called and told the doctor in her department all the details. Everyone knew, but they pretended not to know. . . .

Josef, whom Martha worked with, said, "You'll tell us when you're ready."

The working day passed quickly. She helped everyone with everything, as always. She was an irreplaceable person in the surgical department. They had truly missed her while she was away.

When evening came, Martha decided to call her new acquaintance, Leo, the doctor who had helped her and her brother. He answered immediately when she called; she didn't even have to wait for the second ring. It was as if he had been sitting down and waiting for her to call.

"Hello, Martha," she heard.

"How do you know it's me?"

"I just know," he replied. "How are you doing? How did you get there? How's your brother?" Question after question poured in.

Martha was silent.

"Martha, are you there?" she heard him say.

"I'm sorry," Martha replied. "I'm here. Just thinking. Everything is fine. We got here quickly. Viktor is still at home. But as soon as he recovers, according to him, he will go to war to defend our homeland. He wants to avenge our parents."

Leo said, "Don't let him go. He needs to study. He's still a very young man."

"Young but confident," said Martha. "War is when one family kills another family and it is not clear why."

Leo replied, "Yes, a very correct explanation, but unfortunately, we can't change that. Let's hope it ends soon. Tonight, there was another bombing again. But many residents had already left for the interior of the country. So many people are leaving for Russia. One man said, 'I want to save my family. I don't know what it will be like until Russia returns the territory of Ukraine under its supervision.' I didn't argue with him or try to prove what's true and what's not. Each person makes their own choices and their own independent decisions."

Chapter 4

War

It took several months for Viktor's leg to fully recover. As soon as Martha realized that Viktor had fully recovered, she got him a job in the hospital where she worked.

The war continued. Russia was now bombing all the territories of Ukraine, and many cities and villages were being destroyed. The wounded were being brought to Lviv, and the resettlement of the people of Ukraine to Poland and Germany began.

One morning, the head doctor invited Martha and a few others into his office.

"Good morning," he said. "Today, I had a very serious conversation. Our hospital is moving to Germany. They invited us." He pointed to those present. "We will organize a department for our wounded since we speak Russian, and we will have to learn German. Therefore, they chose young professionals with a prospectus for the work of the future. You have three days to think so we can find replacements for those who will reject this offer."

After the meeting, Martha decided to talk to the head doctor. "I only have one question," she asked.

"Yes, you can stay," the doctor replied.

Sitting down next to his desk, she said, "I will go to Germany with great pleasure. Only I have one request. You know that my parents died from the bombing by Russia, and I have a younger brother whom I must look after. He is still very young. He is only sixteen years old. He is not yet ready for an independent life. And I can't leave him here alone."

She fell silent and waited for an answer from the head doctor.

After thinking for a while, he replied, "No problem. I will negotiate with them. You can take you brother with you."

Martha was very happy that they would both be able to leave the country and start a new life. It could be in Germany or maybe in some other country.

But she had to get away from this horror and violence. She thought, *There's nothing else to keep me here. My parents are with me. I can take them with me, and once I have decided on my place of residence, I will bury them. The house we lived in all those years has been destroyed, and not a single recognizable object remains. Everything has been destroyed; only memories remain. I will take them with me. Viktor and I will build a life in a new country, with new customs and friends, in a new home, where we will create our new memories and traditions.*

Chapter 5
Goodbye, Motherland

It took only a few days to complete the paperwork. Martha and Viktor packed only things that commemorated their happy moments of life, such as a photo album with photos of their childhoods and adolescence with their parents, a few favorite books, and a few other favorite things.

Martha didn't know what else they would need, and she told her brother, "Bring clothes but not many things. Just what you'll need and those that remind you of the happier moments in your life."

But he had almost nothing. He had left their house just to buy bread. All he had were his sneakers, socks, trousers, shirt, and the net in which he had planned to put bread after the purchase.

Martha looked at him and realized that he had almost no possessions. She said, "Don't worry about anything. We'll gain a little bit of everything. The most important thing is that we have each other. It's going to be okay, believe me." She added, "The most important thing is that I have a job, and they will give us an apartment where we can sleep peacefully and not be afraid of bombings."

She hugged her brother. Viktor had changed a lot after what had happened to him. He had become silent. He cried very often. Trying to hide his tears, he turned his face aside.

Martha understood him perfectly well and had tried to create pleasant conditions for him at this transitional stage in his new life. She tried to explain to him and sympathize with him at the same time.

"The most important thing for us now is to learn two languages very quickly," she said. "German, because we are going to Germany, and English, because I will work in a hospital that belongs to America."

Well, the joke turned out to not be funny.

They sat down on the sofa next to each other. According to Russian custom, before going on the road, for good luck, you need to sit for a while, as if to concentrate your thoughts and take as much strength with you as possible.

Martha said, "Well, that's it. Goodbye, my home, my country." She crossed herself and added, "God bless."

She looked at her apartment again, thinking, *Who knows? Maybe it will be preserved. Maybe we will return.* Out loud, she said, "Well, at the moment, I'm saying goodbye to you. Goodbye."

She took their suitcases, while Viktor put his backpack on his shoulder. They left the apartment, and Martha locked her doors.

She had previously told her neighbor that they were going to work in Germany and given her the key to the apartment so she could look after the plants. They needed to be watered once a week. She had also told the neighbor that she could take all the food that was left in the house. The neighbor was a single woman. She was about fifty years old, and she had no children or a husband. If the war reached Lviv, then she would also have to leave the country, but so far, she did not want to go anywhere.

In parting, the neighbor had said, "I was born here, I lived my life here, I will die here, and I will not go anywhere."

It sounded tragic, but on the other hand, it was very brave to accept that a human life could end so cruelly.

Martha and Viktor got into her car and drove to the hospital. There, the group they were traveling with was organized into a column and started moving in the direction of Germany. They went with thoughts and hopes for their difficult but necessary resettlement from Ukraine, where they were born and had lived until today, to Germany, where they would work and live. But they did not know yet for how long.

Martha thought, *Maybe the war will end and we can return, or maybe we will stay in Germany forever.*

Viktor asked, "Will we have our names, or will we be forced to change our names to German?"

"We will have our names. What makes you think that we should change our names?" asked Martha.

"I don't know," Viktor replied. "It's Germany. They probably don't like Russians."

Martha looked at him carefully and replied, "Our mother was born in Russia. We were born in Ukraine. We are Ukrainians, and there is a war in our country now. Russia is advancing on Ukraine. I think that the whole world now sympathizes with our country. What do you think about this?" asked Martha.

She wanted to create soothing thoughts in Viktor's head. She herself did not know—and could not know—how the

German population would perceive immigrants from Ukraine who spoke Russian.

She said, "We have to learn German as quickly as possible. It's our first and most urgent responsibility. We're moving to Germany, so as I understand it, we have to speak their language. I think it will give us a more confident and peaceful life in Germany. They will understand us, and they will respect us for the fact that we will now be Ukrainian Germans. Since we have adopted their language and communicate with them in German, I think. We will cook their German dishes, schnitzel, sauerkraut with sausage. . . . Mom cooked them too. I remember you like them."

"Yes, I love those dishes," Viktor replied.

The conversation dragged on for a long time. Viktor asked question after question, some of which Martha knew the answer to and some she did not.

"We will solve all these issues in the place of our residence," she said. "You and I, we're going to an unknown future, but we have a head on our shoulders and will use it every day, every hour, every minute, okay?"

"Yes, of course," Viktor replied. "But you know that my head cannot do without your head." Looking at Martha, he smiled slightly for the first time.

Martha was very happy about this. She laughed and placed her hand on his head, which held his tied-up hair.

"I agree; one head is good, but two is better. You're my funny little brother, and I understand and love you," she said, pinching his side slightly.

He laughed and said, "Ticklish."

"Ticklish?" repeated Martha, and she pinched him again.

They both laughed for the first time since the death of their parents.

Carrying the two urns with her parents inside, Martha thought to herself, *We are all together for a real minute, and a new life begins for us.*

✶ ✶ ✶

When they reached Munich, they drove up to the appointed meeting point. They were all accommodated in a hotel, and one by one, the families were sent to the apartments belonging to them. The apartments were in different parts of the city but not far from the hospital where they would work.

When Martha opened the door of their new apartment, she was amazed. The apartment had everything one would need for a normal life. It had absolutely everything—furniture and food among other things. They were given one week to get familiar with their new home.

Viktor was amazed by everything he saw, and he asked, "Is this all ours?"

"Yes," replied Martha. "I think it's all for us, and it's all going to be ours if we stay here."

"What do you mean 'if we stay'?" asked Viktor. "Do you think we're going somewhere else?"

"I don't know yet," replied Martha honestly. The hospital she would be working in belonged to America. "I'll let you know as soon as I know all the details. Remember, we have no secrets between us. We must be honest with each other, and we will solve all the issues together, okay?"

"Okay," Viktor agreed.

All week long, they inspected the nearest places around their apartment, stores where they would buy groceries, clothing and shoe stores, and others. Martha bought Viktor everything he needed since he had practically no stuff of his own. She was glad to look after her brother.

Viktor was happy with the purchases, and like a little boy, when he returned home, he immediately tried on his clothes. He began to examine his appearance in the mirror. Wearing new jeans and a new shirt, he looked much older than his age, but he behaved much younger, and Martha liked that. She didn't want him to grow up too fast because of the war.

Martha and Viktor's relocation had a positive effect on them. In the evenings, they both learned German. About six months later, Viktor could speak German without an accent at all.

Martha worked in the hospital, and this helped her to practice her German. She was very purposeful and learned everything she needed for her work easily.

One of the head surgeons noticed this, and she was assigned to the head doctor. His name was Patrick.

I will work under Patrick's guidance, thought Martha.

He had been living in Germany for several years with his wife, Mary. They had three daughters. Ella was sixteen years old, Sue was eighteen, and Margaret was twenty-one.

Patrick decided to invite Martha to dinner, hoping that she and Margaret would be friends. But he could not foresee that Martha's brother, Viktor, would be very glad to meet his family.

One evening, Martha came home from work and said, "Tomorrow, we will go to lunch with our teacher and mentor. He is an amazingly intelligent and patient teacher. He taught me so much in such a short time."

Viktor jokingly asked, "Does he have daughters?"

Martha laughed and replied, "How do you know?"

"You told me that your boss has three daughters. And how old are they? I need friends, as many as possible. You know me; I love new acquaintances, new habits, and new understandings and conversations. I'm just interested in meeting new people," Viktor reasoned.

Martha paid attention to this and thought, *He really perceives each of his new acquaintances in a very interesting way. He seems to study them, their habits, their behaviors, and their gift of speech.* She thought further, *Maybe I need to pay special attention to this. Psychotherapy is a very interesting profession, and Viktor, I suspect, would prepare for that with great pleasure and find success.*

Viktor always gave useful advice to his friends, and everyone respected him for this. Strength and logical thinking—those were exactly what he had in large quantities in his character.

The next day, they were preparing for their lunch trip. Martha noticed Viktor had changed his clothes twice, but she didn't say anything. *I know he wants to leave a positive impression on my boss's daughters*, she thought.

"I'm ready. It's not my habit to be late," Martha said, looking at Viktor.

"I'm ready," he replied, and they went outside.

It turned out that Patrick's house was only a ten-minute drive away.

"Excellent," said Viktor. "Very close. Maybe we go to the same school?"

"Who knows? Maybe," replied Martha.

When they came close to the house, Martha rang the bell on the front door. A voice was heard behind it, and then the door opened. On the other side of the door was a woman. *Probably Mary*, Martha thought.

"Good afternoon," said Martha.

"Good afternoon," Mary replied. "Come in please," she said, switching to English.

Martha and Viktor followed her.

Patrick came out. "Come in. Be at home," he said in pure Russian without any accent.

Martha was surprised, which showed in the expression on her face. "You speak Russian?" she asked.

"Yes, I have known Russian for a very long time. I studied it at an institute in the United States, and I had a friend from Russia. He also studied to be a surgeon, and we helped each other learn the language. He gave me lessons in Russian, and I gave him lessons in English. Come in," he repeated.

Viktor confidently walked into the hall and sat down on the sofa. Martha followed him and sat down next to him.

All three of their daughters came into the room at once, and Patrick introduced them.

"These are my daughters, Ella, Sue, and Margaret."

Viktor got up from the chair, said, "It's very nice to meet you," and sat back down on the sofa.

Martha said, "Do you speak Russian to the girls?"

"No," replied Margaret. "I speak German and English. Sue speaks German and French. Ella speaks five languages, and she is the youngest."

"Wow," said Martha in surprise. "How did you manage to learn five languages at such a young age?"

"I don't know," Ella replied. "Everyone says that I can memorize new words in a new language, and I really like it. Students from many countries come to our school, and I help them. It's the first time I've worked as a translator. Unfortunately, there's no pay," she said and laughed.

"I'm kidding," she added. "It's just interesting for me to meet new students, and I try to help them. I know how difficult and lonely the first time in a new place can be. We moved a lot because of my dad. He was constantly transferred from one place of work to another. That's why I know and have this experience. It is fun for me to help and learn a new language at the same time."

Viktor said, "I suspect that you will now help me learn Russian. I saw you at school."

Ella replied, "I saw you too. When Dad said that Martha and her brother were coming to dinner, I immediately thought it was you because Dad said that you are from Ukraine and I heard everyone at school talking about you and saying that you were from Ukraine. I thought it wasn't a coincidence. It was you, and I was right."

Continuing, she said, "I see you're very good with German. I will teach you English, and you will teach me Russian."

Viktor replied, "My sister is currently learning English. We are good at it. We probably have a knack for foreign languages too."

Mary invited everyone to the table, and they all went. Ella turned out to be a very confident and sociable girl. She immediately asked her mother if she could sit next to Viktor.

"Of course," agreed Mary.

Martha sat between Patrick and Ella.

Lunch was prepared in the German style, and all the dishes had German names. Martha did not yet know all the names, but they tasted excellent.

Each of those present was confident in free communication regardless of age–from Ella, who was only sixteen, to Patrick, who was fifty-one. "Lunch after conversation" or "conversation with lunch" sounds like a correct description of the moment.

Following this lunch, Viktor and Ella became inseparable. After returning from work, Martha heard them speaking Russian, English, and German, and she was very happy that they had become friends.

Martha herself had acquired a new friend: Margaret. They went to museums and went shopping together. Martha taught her to speak Ukrainian and cook Ukrainian dishes while teaching her Russian at the same time.

Patrick and Mary became the closest friends to Martha and Viktor.

Two families became friends, merged in a friendly atmosphere. One family was from Ukraine and one from America, and they met in Germany.

Patrick's family was used to moving from country to country. For them, it was just a normal way of life. But for Martha and Viktor, it was a happy find. They were glad that they had met Patrick and his family.

A year passed, and one day, when Martha came to work, she saw Patrick talking on the phone. She heard him say the name Leo.

What? she thought. *Leo? What Leo?* And then she caught herself thinking, *What if this is my Leo?* She smiled slightly. *No, it can't be. Many men have the same name.*

Having finished the conversation, Patrick approached Martha. He said, "Martha, do you remember a doctor named Leo? He helped you find your parents, and I apologize for reminding you of that terrible, tragic situation."

Martha looked at Patrick and didn't answer for a while. Then, she said, "Yes, I remember. He helped me in the most difficult moment of my life. I will never forget him."

"So," Patrick said, "I just talked to him. He's being transferred to our hospital. He'll be here in a week."

Martha listened carefully and replied, "That's great. He's a very attentive and knowledgeable surgeon."

Patrick noticed that Martha was upset or worried about something, and he could not understand from her behavior what the something was.

He remembered Leo's conversation when he had called him from Mariupol and knew he was interested in Martha. He knew she had moved to Germany and had asked so many questions about her.

Patrick had been honest with him since they had known each other since school years. They had lived near one another, and their parents had been friends for many years. Patrick knew that Leo was in love with Martha, but he didn't want Martha to know.

He thought that perhaps Martha was saddened that Patrick had reminded her of that terrible moment in her life. Then, he thought, *Maybe this will help her accept that moment. It's okay. It's going to be okay. I've known Leo for years. He'll help her forget about everything. No, not forget—just accept as reality.*

When Martha returned home, she was excited that Leo was coming.

When she first met him, she had dreamed of seeing him. But it had been such a long time. Almost two years had passed. Martha did not know what had happened when they met, and for some reason, she was afraid of that moment.

She called Margaret and asked, "Do you have a free minute? I must talk to you. I must talk about what I'm really excited about. I don't even know what to do."

"Calm down," Margaret said. "I'll be right there." And she hung up the phone.

Martha sat worried, thinking, *I have never been this worried, even when passing the state exams at the university. I was not even as worried when I got a job or on my first day of work.*

The doorbell rang, and she went to open it. Margaret was standing on the threshold, looking at Martha with a worried look. "What's the matter?" she asked without crossing the threshold.

"Come in and get ready for the unexpected. What I'm going to tell you doesn't fit into any box," Martha explained. She took Margaret's hands and pulled her inside.

They both sat down at the table in the kitchen.

Martha said, "Tea? Coffee? Wine?"

"What?" Margaret laughed. "Wine? We don't drink wine with you, do we?"

"I know," replied Martha.

"Let's have it," said Margaret.

"I'll start from the beginning. My parents died in the bombing in Mariupol. I went to find out why they weren't answering the phone and found them lying on stretchers under white sheets. He was there," she continued.

"Who is he?" asked Margaret.

"His name is Leo. He is a surgeon, like your father. He was on the front line and helped the wounded. He helped me to cope with life's blow. He took me to the hospital and put me to sleep for the night, during which time he cremated my parents and prepared them for me. That way, I was able to pick them up and take them with me.

"My brother had one leg broken, and he got off well. My mother sent him to the store to buy bread, and as soon as he left the house, the bomb fell right into the house. Mom saved his life.

"In short, Leo was my angel, and he helped me deal with my grief, and then, I don't know what happened. Every time I talked to him, I wanted to hug him and feel his warm soul. A very amazing, wonderful person. I didn't want to part with him. I confess that I had feelings for him, not only as a doctor, a friend, or an angel. I think that I fell in love with him. I'm afraid to say that word because it hasn't happened to me.

"I'll explain quickly. I remember how he moves, how he smiles. I remember his eyes, I remember how I strangely wanted to be in his arms, stand next to him, and just be with him," explained Martha.

She expressed it all so quickly that Margaret was afraid to stop her. But Margaret understood what had happened and what Martha felt now.

"It's scary, isn't it?" Martha asked.

"Are you crazy?" said Margaret. "It's not scary; it's a miracle. I would like to feel this way about a person. This is a gift of nature. Not everyone is capable of that. I envy you."

"Really?" Martha was surprised. "For some reason, I am afraid of these feelings. I'm afraid to show them to him. He's coming this week, and I don't know how to behave." She looked at her friend and waited for an answer.

Margaret replied, "Be yourself, and everything will fall into place. If you are glad to see him, rejoice. If you want to show it to him, show it. But hold back and don't show it until you realize that he's glad to see you too."

"Yes, I think you're right. I should first find out how he feels about me. And then I'll show him my feelings," added Martha. "Maybe he's just trying to help me like a doctor. Who knows what he felt at that moment of first acquaintance," Martha reasoned aloud.

"I agree with you," Margaret replied. "Well, you see, you have found a way out of your delicate state yourself. Good girl," said Margaret. "If you want, I can ask my father to invite him to dinner with us. And of course, you will come late, and I will watch him to see if he waits for you impatiently or just as usual, like he would for everyone else, without much excitement. From his behavior, I can understand his feelings for you."

"Wow, what a good idea," said Martha.

"Yes, that's exactly what we're going to do so we'll understand his condition toward you," Margaret explained.

Martha could not stand it anymore and hugged her friend. "It's so good that I have you," she said.

Margaret replied, "I'm also glad to have a friend as close as you. We trust each other with absolutely everything. Remember, you're going to tell me absolutely everything, okay? Even about your wedding night."

Martha laughed. "Well, girlfriend, if it's not too much for you to tell me about yours."

"I'll tell you about mine," replied Margaret, and they both laughed.

"I had friends, but then, for some reason, we drifted apart. We knew each other, but we didn't have such a close relationship. I can call you my sister, and I'm very happy about that," replied Martha.

Margaret said, "Sister, I hope you'll tell me how you feel about a very nice surgeon," and they both laughed.

Martha felt more confident, calmer, next to Margaret. It was necessary to have a person with whom she could share her thoughts and feelings, from whom she could get advice and understanding in this way. Martha and Margaret had become very close friends.

* * *

At the end of the week, Martha was at work when she heard a conversation on the phone. Patrick was talking to Leo.

He said, "I know you have one week to get into your house and then go straight to work. I need extra hands. We've got a large influx of wounded. And I'd also like to invite you to our house this Friday for dinner. Mary said she missed you."

What? Martha thought. Mary knows him too? They must have known each other for years.

At lunchtime, she called Margaret. Martha told her that she had overheard the conversation. She talked either with fright or with delight in her voice; it was very difficult to understand.

Margaret said, "Yes, he came. I heard Dad and Mom talking. My mother is his cousin. Leo and I are related; I forgot to tell you that. So if you marry him, we'll be close friends and relatives."

"Marry?" replied Martha. "Margaret, you scare me. I am afraid of his presence, and you say I will marry him? What is the matter with you?"

Margaret continued, "You're afraid of his presence because you love him. Haven't you figured it out yet? Wake up, sister; you're head over heels in love with him."

Martha replied, "I won't go to dinner on Friday. I'm afraid to show it to him and all those present. It will bring inconvenience to those around me."

Margaret stopped her. "Hey, listen to me carefully. You'll be late for dinner as agreed. I must tell you, I told my mother about our conversation, and she's very happy for both of you. She said that Leo is constantly interested in you, how you are, and what you are, so I think he feels the same way you feel about him. Leo told my father that he was going crazy from all this time apart. He's afraid that you will meet someone. He tried to complete his transfer as quickly as possible. I have to admit to you that it's very difficult to transfer from the front line. So, your pigeon has flown to you to build his nest of love."

Martha laughed. "You speak as you sing, almost in verse. Okay, thank you for the information. Please stop torturing me. I can't find a place for myself."

"Okay, I'm going to your house after work. 6:00 p.m.," she added. "See you later." And she hung up.

Martha sighed deeply, either from comfort or from fear. But now that she knew Leo had only transferred to Germany because she was here, she calmed down a little. It put a smile on her face without her even noticing.

She thought, *So, my feelings did not let me down. He also has more than friendly feelings for me.* She remembered his look, his embrace, and the attention he had paid to her. "Thank you, God," she said aloud.

Suddenly, Martha came to her senses and noticed there were many nurses and doctors around her.

"'Thank you, God' for what?" asked the nurse sitting next to her.

"For reporting the result of my wounded," she said. "He will live."

She got up from her computer and walked into the hallway. *There's still time before the operation. I have to concentrate*, she thought.

She took the patient's card, read it carefully again, and said aloud, "I'm ready for surgery."

She went to the operating room and began to prepare everything necessary. She checked everything many times to make sure she made no mistakes. It was her routine every day.

*　*　*

In the morning, she got up early. Viktor said that he would like to stay at his friend's place. They would play chess, and his friend had asked him to sleep over. Martha agreed, and Viktor packed his necessary things after breakfast.

Schwartz, his friend, came to pick him up at about one o'clock in the afternoon. Martha knew him and where he lived. She was acquainted with his parents. They both worked at the school where Viktor studied. Schwartz's father was the school principal, and his mother was a chemistry and biology teacher.

When Viktor left, Martha began to clean the apartment. She had only two days off, today and tomorrow. *I have a lot of things to do. Clean the apartment, do some shopping. Maybe I should buy a new dress for when I meet Leo.* She caught herself thinking, *I didn't think about what he will look like for a long time.*

Yes, she confirmed, *I will go to the store and buy myself a new dress.*

After finishing cleaning and laundry, she was ready to go to the store when, suddenly, the doorbell rang. *Who could it be? I'm not waiting for anyone,* she thought.

She went to open the door. Looking through the peephole, she was surprised. No, not surprised; she was amazed. It was Leo.

She was standing on the other side of the door and did not know what to do. The bell rang again.

She thought, *I will not open it for him. Let him think that I am not at home.* But her hands opened the doors for some reason. They stood and looked at each other in silence, and it only took them one minute to make a very serious decision.

Leo crossed the threshold of the front door, closed it behind him, and said, "Hello, dear, I can't wait any longer. I have decided that I should see you today."

He came very close to her, and Martha looked at him silently without blinking. Leo hugged her and held her tightly to him. So much so that Martha had to take a deep breath.

She said, "I don't want to wait any longer either."

After these words, his lips touched her cheek and then her eyes, and he began to kiss her. The kiss was tender and greedy at the same time. Martha felt like she had been waiting for this for a very long time, and she put all her feelings into their first kiss. Martha had dreamed about it when they met in Mariupol. But after two years, she had begun to lose hope that it would ever happen.

After the very long first kiss, Leo said, "What have you done to me? After I saw you in Ukraine, I couldn't stop thinking about you every day. From today on, you're mine. I'm not going to give you to anyone," and he kissed her again. Then, he took her in his arms and carried her to the bedroom.

Martha laughed. "No, not in this room. This is my brother's room."

Leo asked, "Is he home?"

"No," replied Martha. "He'll be back tomorrow for lunch, and after that, we'll go to Patrick's dinner, where we're supposed to meet you."

"Yes, I know, but I can't be next to you in the same city and be without you. What if you get the time to meet someone? I decided that I should see you today."

Martha laughed. "I know a lot of people, but they're just not you. You have done something to me too. I can't forget the look of your eyes, the touch of your hands, and, most importantly, that you were with me in the most difficult moment of my life. And I felt protected from the whole world."

Leo put her on the bed. They kissed each other again, and suddenly, he asked, "Martha, will you be my wife?"

Martha was surprised by such a question. "What?" she asked.

"What's wrong with that? I'll let you decide in a few weeks. Because I already know that I want to marry you and I'm not going to change my mind. You gave my heart a feeling that I have never experienced, and I don't want to lose it," he said.

He began to kiss her again, and they made love after love.

After a few hours together, Martha no longer doubted her answer. They were lying in bed. He held her in his arms and did not want to let her go, not for a second, and they fell asleep.

When Martha woke up, she slowly left the room, a smile shining on her face. She went to the kitchen and began to prepare dinner. She knew that Leo and she were both hungry. She made cutlets and fried potatoes, and she already had freshly baked poppy seed buns.

She saw Leo standing in the doorway, staring at her, and she asked, "How long have you been spying here?"

"About five minutes," he answered. "I admire you. What did you cook? It smells very tasty all over the house. I was forced to come to the kitchen, for like a little boy, I followed the smell of food."

Martha replied, "Do you mean I woke you up?"

"No, not you," Leo replied. "I was woken up by the smell of food, which is, of course, your fault. Yes, I'm hungry, very hungry," he said. He came up and hugged her from behind and kissed her neck, her hair, and her shoulders.

Martha said, "If you keep going like this, the dinner will get cold."

He laughed. "You're reading my mind." He took her in his arms, and they were back in bed.

It was already dark outside when they finally sat down at the table, and they were both very hungry.

Leo said, "I'm eating a homemade dinner. When was the last time?" He paused, thinking, and then said, "A very, very long time ago."

They ate a deliciously cooked dinner and talked about work and about Patrick and Mary.

Leo said, "Mary wanted to study to be a chef before she met Patrick. But after they got married, she decided that she would be a wife and mother and that she knew enough about cooking. She now has a more serious job: to raise children and love them and help them be respectful, intelligent people. Mary is my cousin."

"I know," replied Martha. "Margaret already told me about it, and she also told me that you grew up together and that Mary always looked after you because you were a troublemaker."

"No," Leo replied. "I was just curious. I wanted to learn as much as possible everywhere and about everything."

"Yes," agreed Martha. "She told me all about your actions and behavior."

"Okay, I'll beat Margaret!" he joked. "What else has she told you about me?"

"A lot about how you wanted to run away from home, but when you reached the bus stop, you realized that it was better at home than surrounded by strangers and returned. Your cousin was punished for that, not you, because she didn't keep track of your escapes."

"What?" Leo said. "I don't remember that she was punished. I must apologize to her."

Leo stayed overnight and only went home the next morning.

Laughing, he said, "I have to go home and get ready for an unexpected encounter with you."

"Are we going to pretend that we didn't see each other, or are we confessing everything?" Martha asked.

Leo replied, "Let's first try to pretend that we just met and see how long we last."

"I suspect that, in five minutes, everything will be known from our behavior."

Leo left, and Martha began to try on her dresses since she hadn't had time to buy a new one yesterday.

Viktor returned and noticed that there were two plates and two of everything on the kitchen table.

He asked, "Has Leo been here yet?"

"What?" asked Martha in surprise. "How do you know that?"

"You forgot to wash the dishes in the kitchen. And I've never seen you try out your dresses before. You usually get ready ten minutes before you leave the house."

Martha was surprised at her brother's observation; she did not know how to answer.

Viktor helped her, saying, "I remember him. We met in Mariupol. I saw how he was taking care of you, and I saw how you both looked at each other. I realized even then that this was not the last meeting with him, and I was right." Smiling, Viktor added, "It's okay, sister. I won't tell anyone about it. It will be our secret."

He looked at his sister and was very surprised by her reaction. "Martha, what's wrong?" he asked.

Martha sat down on the sofa and said, "Come here. Sit next to me. I want to share with you exactly what is happening."

Viktor approached her and sat down next to her.

Martha first asked, "What dress do you think I'm going to wear for dinner?"

"Turquoise," he replied without hesitation.

"You and I have the same tastes," replied Martha. "Listen, he came last night, and we've been together all this time. He left this morning, and he asked me to marry him. . . . That's what worries me. I don't know him at all. Leo saw me for only one day when I was completely out of my mind, and we hardly spoke. We were only looking at each other. Can you really explain our feelings with a look?"

"Yes, you can," Viktor replied. "Ella and I, we don't talk about love and loyalty, but I know that she loves me, and I love her. You know, Martha, sometimes, you love a person without telling him about it. Sometimes, people tell you, 'I love you,' but their feelings are not so strong. They say these words and try to convince themselves of what they're saying."

Martha looked at her brother all this time in silence. When he stopped, she said, "You're only eighteen years old. Where did you get such experience and reasoning from? You are my little brother, and you just explained my feelings to me so easily and quickly that I now have no doubt about what answer I will give to Leo."

Viktor looked at her with a smile. "So we will have a wedding soon?" he asked. "Ella and I decided to go to the same institute after school. We will study to become psychiatrists. We will open our own clinic and work together. You know, we will also get married but only after graduation. Mom, she's just the most amazing girl I know."

'What?" asked Martha. "What did you call me?"

"Wow," said Viktor. "I called you Mom. . . . You know, I'm so used to you taking care of me like our mom."

"That's the biggest compliment to me," replied Martha.

"I'm very glad I have you. You're my only relative. That's why Ella and I will get married. We will have many children; we decided so. So that, when we die, they don't feel alone." Viktor looked at Martha. "And I said I would advise you and your husband to have at least three children too or even more. I want to have many relatives. I am very happy that you and Leo will be married. I immediately liked him. As soon as I woke up in that hospital, I saw he has a very kind heart."

"Thanks for the tips," Martha replied. She kissed her brother on the top of his head as she got up from the sofa. "I will go and make you breakfast, or rather, dinner."

"Something very light. I'm not hungry, and we'll go to an early dinner soon. They invited us to four o'clock, didn't they?" Viktor asked.

"Yes, at 4:00 p.m.," replied Martha from the kitchen.

"I'll be in my room," he said, and he walked in the direction of his room.

Suddenly, the doorbell rang. He stopped.

Martha asked, "Who are you waiting for?"

"No one," he said. *Strange. Who could it be?* he thought as he walked to the door. He peeped through the glass in the door and saw a stranger behind the door. He thought, *I should not open the door. I should go to the kitchen.*

Entering the kitchen, he said, "Some stranger is here."

Martha answered, "Let's not open. He probably has the wrong address."

There was another knock on the door.

Martha decided to see who it was. She went very carefully to the door and looked out of the window. *No, I don't know who it is,* she thought and immediately and quietly walked away from the door.

Martha and Viktor sat at the kitchen table. Viktor was eating his breakfast/lunch, and Martha just sat next to him and watched her brother. After he called her Mom, she had begun to admire him as her own son. She hadn't noticed it before, but she had been doing it all the time since the death of her parents.

After finishing breakfast, Viktor said, "I'll go take a little nap. I didn't sleep almost all night."

Martha washed the dishes. *I also did not sleep all night.* Then, she corrected herself and thought happily, *Almost all night. But I don't regret it, and for some reason, I don't feel tired.*

After removing everything from the table and washing the dishes, she went into the hall, and she noticed that something was sticking out from under the front door.

She went to the door. First, she looked out the window; there was no one there. Then, she opened the door, and there was a letter in front of the door. The man from before had probably tried to put it under the door, but the door was very tightly installed, so he could insert only a small piece of the corner of the envelope.

Martha took the letter, examined it, and read it. On the envelope was written her address and her name. She closed the door and went to sit on the sofa, and only then did she open the envelope.

Inside, there was a piece of paper folded in four parts. She unfolded it and began to read:

> Hello, Martha, I hope this letter will find you. I'm your mother's brother. I know we don't know each other, but when I found out what happened to your parents, I began to look for you and your brother, and so, I was given this address.

"My mother's brother?" she said aloud. *I never heard my mother say that she had a brother. Why didn't she tell us about him?* Martha thought. *The young man who brought the letter cannot be her brother. He is very young; he must be this brother's son. Do I have relatives in Germany?*

"What a surprise," she said aloud.

Well, why didn't my mother and he communicate? I don't like it. Why didn't they communicate? In her thoughts arose question after question.

She began to read further. Her detailed address was written there, as were instructions for how to get from Martha's house to the house of this new relative.

> My name is Pawel. I would very much like to meet you. I am already at an old age, and I would like to meet you before I die. I know you have many questions for me, but I will explain everything to you and hope for your forgiveness. The war changed the whole course of my life. I hope that you have understood that our father, your mother's grandfather, did not return to Russia after the war.

He stayed in Germany. He was wounded, and he met a woman and decided to stay. He wrote a letter to your grandmother and explained everything to her.

I hope she didn't get this letter, thought Martha.

"Oh my gosh," she said out loud. *I don't know anything about it. My grandmother, Anna, said that her husband, my grandfather, died in the war, that she did not know what happened to him. She said that he was missing. It's so good that she didn't get this letter*, Martha thought. *It's much better to think that her husband died as a hero than to read a letter from him explaining to her that he met a woman and decided to stay in Germany. So this man is not my mother's brother. He is a half-brother since they have a common father—well, another mother. How sad.*

I don't know if I want to meet him, she continued to contemplate. *My grandfather left my grandmother and his child and did not return to them. I wouldn't want to know him.*

Martha decided to tell this story to her brother and future husband. *We must discuss this issue, and only then will I decide whether I need to get acquainted with him*

The letter concluded with the fact that he would be happy to meet them, and at the end, he had written a phone number.

Martha looked at the clock. It was 3:00 p.m. It was time to wake Viktor. He needed to be ready for dinner at Patrick's.

A very important day, thought Martha. *Let's see what happens.*

She went to her brother's room and quietly shook his shoulder. She said in his ear, "Wake up, dear. Viktor, it's time to get up. You need time to prepare." She stroked his head, leaned over him, and kissed him on the nose. She loved her brother so much. *Only Viktor is my relative now*, she thought.

Viktor opened his eyes. "Okay, I'll go shower." He got up from the bed and walked slowly in the direction of the shower.

Martha also went to prepare for a meeting with her future husband and his relatives.

She wore a turquoise dress, like her brother had advised. Looking at herself in the mirror, she was surprised: the dress sat on her very attractively. The color of the dress was very suitable for her skin tone, and the style of the dress showed off her flawless figure.

Thank you, Viktor, she thought. *He must've remembered that this dress suits me very well. My brother is gradually turning from a young man into a grown man.*

I am very happy to have such a brother. He is my angel. He gives me strength, and I know that I should be with him since he has no one but me. He brings me joy when I see his success at school and his correct understanding of various actions, she continued reflecting happily. *Maybe Leo and I really should have a lot of children. It is very difficult and lonely to be without relatives around you for company, for support, and for joy. Close people are called close because they are the closest to you. Almost the same blood flows in our veins, as we have the same DNA.*

Viktor left the room and announced to her that he was ready. Martha looked at him. He was dressed very simply but tastefully. He had put on black trousers, a white shirt, and a black tie.

"Wow!" said Martha. "You're such an interesting young man. You probably have a lot of fans at school?"

"No, I have a lot of friends and only one fan; that's my Ella," he replied.

"That's enough," replied Martha. "Well, we only need one forever. Like Mom and Dad." She didn't say anything about the letter. It was for another time, another day.

They left for dinner, and Martha did as she and Margaret had agreed. She was a little late and had to tell Viktor about their plan so that he would not ruin it.

They drove up to Patrick's house. He had a very comfortable and large house. There was enough space for everyone, including his three daughters, and there was even a large guest house, which stood not far from the house.

Out of habit, Viktor rang the doorbell, and then he knocked twice, which announced that Viktor was here. This sign was known to everyone in the house except Leo.

Ella opened the door. She hugged Viktor, then noticed that he was not alone. She became shy and invited them into the house.

She led them directly into the dining room. Almost everyone was already sitting at the table. Except for Leo. He stood in the corner, as if being punished. From this place, he could see the front door, and he watched everybody that came in. Two more couples from the clinic where Patrick worked had been invited as well.

Leo immediately walked over to Martha. He held out his hand to her and said, "I'm glad to see you. You look sensational."

Martha smiled and replied, "Thank you."

Margaret watched them.

"I think we've seen each other before," she whispered, leaning in by Leo's ear.

He smiled. "Yes, I told them about my visit. Of course, I didn't say all the details out loud, but what I couldn't do was wait longer for our meeting. I told them that we met for dinner and, over a glass of wine, remembered our first day of meeting."

Martha, smiling in response, said, "It's good that we don't have to deceive. I'm very bad at doing it. My mother could immediately determine that I was cheating. She was surprised. I can now immediately determine just like her. When Viktor lies, I give him a special look, and he understands that I know that he is cheating, and he will immediately lay everything out without stopping, afraid to miss something."

Martha and Leo sat next to each other. Viktor, of course, sat next to Ella. Patrick sat next to Leo, and Mary was a force between the wives of friends. Margaret sat on the opposite side of the table from where Martha and Leo were sitting. She watched every move.

Smiling, Martha thought, *Margaret is trying to understand our relationship.*

The dinner was surprisingly interesting. Patrick introduced Leo to everyone present and began to talk about all his achievements in the field of medicine. Over time, his childhood and adolescent memories came up too.

When they lived near each other, Mary and Leo had been inseparable friends. Many had thought they were brother and sister.

"We are brother and sister," Mary chimed in. "I remember one very serious incident in our life. Leo had decided that he would go to live in another country. We were then ten or eleven years old. I asked him which country he would like to go. He replied, 'To Russia.' 'To Russia? Why?' I asked him. 'Russia is the largest country.' 'Well, so what?' I ask him. He answered, 'In order to study all of Russia, I need to live for many years in the territory of Russia. Until I learn everything, I will travel and get acquainted with various traditions and people in the territory of Russia. The language of the Russians is special. I tried to translate a few sentences, and I confess to you, I couldn't. Russian sentences are very long, and when I translated them into English, the sentences turned out to be very short.'"

"I couldn't understand how it was possible, which is why I wanted to go to Russia," Leo added to the story. "Because I didn't understand it and I'm always worried about what I don't understand. That happened to me many times when I was a child."

Mary added, "Yes, you were very curious."

With a smile on his face, Leo replied, "No, not curious; most likely inquisitive."

"Yes. Inquisitive and curious," she added, laughing.

"Okay," Leo agreed. "I'm curious. I want to know what I want to know. That curiosity led me to medical school."

"Enough," Ella said. "All about Leo. I understand my father likes to introduce his friends, but I want to have a different topic. We need to discuss very serious issues. For example, what do you think about what is happening in Ukraine? Do you think that the Russian government should return the territory of Ukraine to Russia, or will the Russians decide to conquer Poland and such and such after that?"

All those present entered the conversation, and after a long conversation, everyone concluded that Russia had set the task of reclaiming all the countries that had seceded from Russia—Ukraine, Belarus, Estonia, Latvia, Kazakhstan, Uzbekistan, and so on.

After dinner, Martha and Leo decided that it would be better if they took a break today. Martha invited him to dinner tomorrow.

He asked, "What if you come to my place? I'll cook my favorite dish for lunch. I'll cook what I know." A mysterious smile crossed his face.

"Okay," Martha agreed. "See you tomorrow."

He kissed her on the cheek since Viktor was sitting in the car and waiting for his sister.

Arriving home, Viktor said, "I think that the wedding will take place very soon. He will blow the dust off you. I think that, after my professional review, I am not mistaken to conclude that he will be a wonderful husband and father."

Martha smiled and said, "Thank you, Viktor."

Viktor went to his room; he would probably be on the phone with Ella. Martha decided to watch a movie. She began to go through the channels on TV, and suddenly, she stopped at the news.

The news was covering Ukraine. It showed many cities that were destroyed, wiped off the face of the earth, including Mariupol. It was very difficult to determine which part of the city they were showing.

What a pity about my city, where I lived with my family all those years, our happy years of life. No one imagined or could have imagined that, in a few decades, there would be a war. The Russians will kill Russians. How cruel and stupid it sounds.

Martha switched to another channel. She thought of her parents. They were still with them in the house, the very beautiful porcelain urns standing on the fireplace nearby. She never distinguished between them. They were her mom and dad, both during life and after death.

"You'll be together," she said aloud.

She got up from the sofa and approached them. Then, she put her right hand on the urn with her mother and her left hand on the urn where her father was. She thanked them both, as if feeling their presence, touching her parents. . . .

"I don't want to part with you," she said. "I don't know when I'll make this decision. But for now, you will be with us."

She told her parents that she had met a man named Leo and that she loved him. "He proposed to me. I haven't given him my consent yet, but I've decided that I'll marry him. He really loves me, and I love him." After standing for a few minutes in silence, she said, "Good night, my dear mom and dad," and went to her room.

The next day, Viktor went to meet with friends, and Martha went to Leo's for lunch.

Leo had been busy preparing dinner all morning, cooking his favorite dish: pasta with meatballs.

Martha had made a cucumber salad and taken it with her. She still adhered to the Russian tradition of not entering a new house of new friends empty-handed.

After driving up to the house where Leo lived, she approached his home and stopped. For some reason, she was afraid to cross the threshold.

Wow, she thought. *Is it because I love him, or is it because I'm doing something wrong?* These words made her soul even more frightened.

A strong emotion bubbled up from within her. For some reason, she felt that she was taking the wrong step. She stepped away from Leo's house. She ran to her car and got behind the wheel. Trying to breathe as deeply as possible, she tried to calm down. But nothing helped. She got out of the car and began to walk along the sidewalk from one side to the other.

The windows of the house overlooked the parking lot where her car was parked. Martha didn't know that, nor did she know that Leo was watching her. He had decided to look out of the window, as Martha was late. Going to the window, he had seen that she was walking on the sidewalk. It was clear that she was somehow upset. Her face was slightly pale, and as a doctor, he immediately realized that she was having a panic attack.

He thought about whether it would be better to go out and calm her down or give her time alone to calm down with her thoughts. He looked out the window, watching her, and decided it would be better if he went out and helped her. He was afraid that she would get in the car and drive away—which was exactly what happened while he was thinking it. Martha got into the car and drove away. He was very upset, but there was nothing he could do.

Everything that had happened between Martha and Leo happened so quickly that Martha was left in confusion. In her feelings, she was not sure that she loved him. She returned home, and she wanted to call him. *But what can I tell him? How can I explain what I am feeling?* she thought.

The phone rang.

It's Leo, Martha thought. She took a deep breath and went to the phone, staring at it, not knowing whether to answer or not. She did not answer, and the phone stopped ringing. It switched to the answering machine.

"Martha, it's Leo. What happened? You are late for my deliciously cooked lunch." He tried to speak calmly, as if he didn't know anything. "What happened? Maybe you're on your way already? I'm waiting for you here. See you soon," he said and hung up.

Martha sat down on the sofa and covered her face with her hands. But she did not cry; she was just frozen in some incomprehensible state.

She thought quickly, very quickly, *No, I'm not ready for such a relationship.* She fell silent.

The phone rang again. This time, she got up from the couch, went to the phone, picked it up, and said, "Yes, I'm listening."

"Martha, is that you?" she heard. "What's the matter? The food is getting cold."

Martha listened to him in silence. When he too fell silent, she explained to him, "Leo, I must confess to you. I'm not ready for such a relationship. I'm not sure about everything that happened before. I think we need to start all over again. I want to be friends first, to get to know each other. I need more time to make such a serious decision."

She was trying to speak in a calm and confident voice, but her whole body was trembling from everything that was happening.

Leo told her, "Martha, you don't have to apologize. I understand everything perfectly. I agree to everything, to all your conditions. We will be friends, as you wish, for however long you decide. But today, I've cooked a very tasty dish, and I think there's nothing wrong with having lunch together."

Martha smiled slightly. *He always knows how to calm me down*, she thought. "All right," she agreed. "I'll be there."

"See you soon," he replied.

"See you soon," Martha said.

She got up from the table and drove back to meet Leo. Driving up to his house, she was afraid that the same thing would happen, but Leo was waiting for her in the parking lot.

He said, "Well done. We're going to eat now. I'm so hungry."

He offered her his hand, and she took it. They went into the house together. She saw that the table was set with style—candles, wine, and very beautiful plates.

He sat her down at the table. "Do you want me to put away the candles and the wine?" he asked.

Martha replied, "No. Leave them be. It's very nice of you, very tasteful."

"I'm going to bring our dinner," he said, and he went to the kitchen.

Only now did Martha look around; the apartment was very cozy. Leo came back with a pot that had pasta in it, and then he brought the meatballs in a large plate.

He boasted, "This is something I love to cook, and I hope you like it." He put pasta and a few balls of meat on her plate.

Martha only now remembered and said, "I forgot my salad. I made a cucumber salad."

"It is okay. Another time."

"No, the salad is in the car," Martha said.

"Let me pick up the salad," Leo said.

"Okay," she agreed and handed him her car keys.

Leo left the house, and Martha began to look at the apartment again. She got up from the table and went to the window, and then she thought, *What if he saw me rushing from side to the side and walking on the sidewalk? Well, if he saw, he realized that I was not ready for such a close relationship.*

She saw Leo take the salad out of the car and walk toward home. She waved to him, and he responded in kind.

She sat down at the table when he returned. Leo put out some salad for her, opened a bottle of wine, and poured it into glasses. He said, "To our new beginning, to friendship."

After these words, Martha raised her glass and said, "To friendship."

They both drank a little and began to eat a deliciously prepared lunch, just as Leo had said. They ate in silence.

After a few minutes, he said, "It shouldn't be so stressful. Let's talk about what you usually like to talk about."

"What do I like to talk about?" asked Martha.

"About your relocation to another country. How do you like it here?"

And they switched to a conversation that did not include the word "love" or anything about relationships. They talked only about the clinic, Germany, and the bunch of friends that they had.

After that, the situation really changed. Martha began to feel much freer, without any feelings of pressure from their relationship.

* * *

Lunch became a normal way of life. They met for dinner at Leo's house or Martha's. They went to the cinema, to the theater, and even to the circus from Ukraine. Martha and Leo became close friends, and Martha liked that.

One evening, when he was having dinner at Martha's house, Viktor invited Ella.

Martha said, "I've been wanting to talk to you about a very serious and unexpected conversation for a very long time."

She took out the letter from her relative who lived in Germany. At first, she reminded Viktor that a stranger had come to them and said that she had found this letter under their door. Then, she read it aloud.

"I would like to hear the opinion of each of you about what we should do, to meet with him or not. We need to weigh it all up and discuss it because it's very important. It's going to affect our lives," she said.

Viktor and Ella were watching Martha all this time, listening attentively.

Leo asked, "Can I give you my opinion?"

"Yes, of course," agreed Martha and Viktor.

Leo sighed heavily, looked at Martha, and began, "I think you need to get to know him. He is your relative. You don't know the whole story about why his father stayed. I think you need to know all the details; that's my opinion."

"Martha, I think this is the right advice," Viktor agreed. "He was looking after our family when the war began, so he still worries about his relatives."

"I think we should honestly tell him the whole truth about what happened to us, what we feel at the present moment," Martha said. "How are we going to do it? Are we going to call him and invite him to visit us, or do we have to go to see him?"

Leo said to her, "I think you should call him and invite him to come here alone. Let him tell us everything, and then we will decide whether we should meet his family or not."

Martha said, "I think he can't come alone since he sent his son to us."

"Yes, it's true; he probably can't go alone."

Viktor suggested, "Ella and I can pick him up. As Ella knows the city very well, we will have no problem finding his house."

"Very good offer. We will do so," said Martha. "I'll call him, and we'll arrange a meeting."

They discussed which day would be convenient for everyone, and they chose three days from then, just in case Pawel was busy on one of these days.

Martha went to the phone at what she was sure was a convenient and suitable time to call. Leo and Viktor were sitting next to each other at the table when she dialed the phone number specified in the letter.

The call was answered very quickly. It was a woman's voice. Martha could not guess who it was. *Time will put everything in its place*, she thought. "Good afternoon," Martha said. "Can I talk to Pawel?"

The woman asked, "May I know who is asking?"

"My name is Martha," she replied. "I received a letter from him."

"Yes, yes, I know. We wrote the letter together. I'll get him now," she replied with excitement in her voice.

Then, there was silence on the other side of the phone. About a minute later, Martha heard a voice that sounded like an old man with a squeaky note.

"Hello, Martha," he said in Russian but with an accent. "I'm very glad you called. I prayed and hoped you would call. Thank you for giving me the opportunity to explain everything to you. All these years, I have been thinking about how this meeting would take place and when. And where. And with whom. And finally, I will see you."

Martha said, "I suggest that you don't come to us. My brother, Viktor, will come to you. We've decided that we would like to get to know you and talk to you first. And then we'll get to know your whole family, if you don't mind."

"Yes, I agree. When and where?" he asked.

"We have three days. Which one is better for you?" she asked, and she named the days. *He talked to his wife*, Martha thought.

They decided on next Saturday at 2:00 p.m. Viktor and Ella would pick him up. Martha hung up the phone and immediately sank down on the couch with a deep breath.

"It wasn't that easy to talk to him, but the woman's voice somehow worried me," Martha said. "Probably because I think my grandfather decided to stay and leave my grandmother and marry another woman. I think it's going to be hard for me to come to terms with it." She looked at Viktor and Leo with a questioning look.

They were both silent.

"Why are you silent?" she asked.

Leo replied, "You were very confident, very precise. You've made a good impression for our family."

"Thank you for that," Viktor added. "You're not just a surgical nurse; you'd make a great lawyer or diplomat."

Martha replied, "Why did you decide to play a joke on me? I was trembling like an aspen leaf during our entire conversation."

"What?" asked Leo in surprise. "But according to you, we shouldn't say that." He looked at Viktor. They were both smiling.

"Stop mocking me; it's not funny. I was really worried."

"I'm sorry," Leo replied. "Be a little kinder to him when he comes."

"You're going to be here, aren't you? Maybe you can ask him questions. I will only listen and draw conclusions, but well, after my grandfather's act, I would say he is very bold. It will be difficult for me to characterize him positively."

"Don't worry, my dear sister. We'll all be here together, and together, we will listen and ask any questions we have," Viktor said. "I won't miss a word he says. This will be real psychological preparation for our future profession. It will be just homework for Ella and me. Preparation for our very professional and very serious work."

An hour later, Viktor left to visit Ella. Martha and Leo were left alone. They decided to watch a movie. Leo made popcorn. They sat down on the couch and turned on the TV. The film was called *The Story of a Couple in Love*. The couple in the movie broke up for a few years but eventually met again, and they came together for many years of their life.

Leo said, "The part of the movie where they broke up reminds me of us. Now I must wait for you to come back to me."

Martha looked at him and said, "I think I'm going to pick up my suitcase soon and move in with you like in the movie."

"I'll be very happy," replied Leo. He hugged Martha very carefully and effortlessly and kissed her. He was afraid to scare her again with his actions.

But Martha got up from the sofa, took his hand, and pulled him to the bedroom. Leo immediately took her in his arms, and they disappeared behind the door.

One can imagine that it was like a second wedding night, but now, Martha did not doubt her decision. She loved him. And she decided that it was time to change their friendship to a more serious relationship.

Leo, of course, was very happy. So, with the transition of the relationship, he was in heaven from happiness. He was very patient and had waited for this moment. He had been sure that, one day, he would make them happy, and now, that day had come.

He didn't say anything to Martha, but he had already prepared a ring for her. This ring had belonged to his mother. He'd had it for a long time, saving it for the woman who would make him happy, and of course, he would make his beloved the happiest woman on Earth too.

The day of meeting the relatives came, and Viktor and Ella went to pick up Pawel. It turned out that he lived near Leo, in the same area of the city.

After arriving at the house, Viktor went to the door and rang the bell. A girl immediately opened the door. She was about the same age as Viktor.

"Good afternoon," he said. "My name is Viktor. I am Martha's brother."

"Good afternoon," the girl replied. "My name is Anna. Dad named me after your grandmother."

"Really?"

"Come in," said the girl.

"No, I'll wait for Pawel in the car," Viktor replied. "I'm not alone. My fiancé came with me, and I don't want to leave her alone."

"Okay," replied Anna. "I'll go get my father. I'll tell him you're here."

"Thank you," Viktor replied and walked toward the car.

He got in the car, and they waited for Pawel. "He has a daughter" Viktor said. "Her name is Anna, like my grandmother. I think he has a son, a young man, who brought the letter."

As soon as Viktor finished his sentence, they saw Anna and Pawel leaving the house. They were walking in the direction of the car.

Viktor came out to meet him. He approached Pawel, stretched out his hand, and said, "My name is Viktor, and this is my fiancé, Ella."

Pawel replied, "I'm very glad to meet you. You can't imagine how happy I am. I've been dreaming of meeting you for a long time. I thank God for answering my prayers and dreams."

Viktor opened the car doors for Pawel and then for Ella and got behind the wheel himself. Then, they drove home.

Pawel said, "It turns out we live very close. It's convenient for us, for our future."

Viktor thought, *He already thinks of the future. I hope that Martha and I can forgive our grandfather for his cruel, daring act.*

It took only fifteen minutes to get home. After driving up to the parking lot, Viktor opened the door for Pawel and Ella.

Then, he stood next to Pawel and suggested, "Okay, it's time for a very important and serious meeting, so let's be honest. When Martha learned that our grandfather was so cruel to our grandmother, she did not want to meet you. But her fiancé explained to her that she should not make serious decisions without knowing the whole truth."

"Yes, I agree," replied Pawel.

They walked toward the house. Viktor opened the doors, and they all went inside the apartment.

Martha had laid the table and prepared tea, coffee, and various pastries. The conversation would not be easy, so she had decided that they would talk without wine.

Leo went to meet Pawel and introduced himself. "My name is Leo. I am Martha's fiancé," he said confidently. Now, Pawel knew his position on their relationship.

"It's a pleasure to meet you," replied Pawel.

Leo said, "This is my fiancé, Martha, Viktor's sister. They are the children of Maria and Ivan. Come in. Make yourself comfortable at the table. What do you prefer to drink: tea, coffee, or wine?"

Pawel replied, "I think the wine will give me more courage for our conversation."

Martha brought two bottles of wine, white and red.

She asked, "Would you like to have white or red?"

"Red," replied Pawel, and Martha poured him a glass of red wine.

Then, they sat down at the table. Viktor drank tea, and Ella drank coffee. Leo and Martha poured themselves red wine too.

It seemed as if this was the negotiation table of two responsible parties, like two countries, Ukraine and Germany—or maybe Russia and Germany because the conversation would be about their grandfather, not their parents. He was born in Russia and lived in Russia before the war with Germany.

Leo suggested, "Pawel, you start our conversation. Tell us what happened to Grandpa Petro."

"Yes, of course," replied Pawel. "Where to start . . . ?"

"Start with how he met Berta?" Martha said, finally joining the conversation. Until then, she had only listened and watched Pawel. Everyone heard anger and resentment in her voice on behalf of her grandmother Anna.

Pawel began, "I know you're mad at Petro, but if you find out everything that's happened, I hope you'll change your mind.

"So, since he met Berta. As you know, he spoke German because he worked as a teacher at a school. When he was wounded and unconscious, for some reason, he was placed in a hospital in Germany. Berta worked there as a nurse. He didn't say that he was Russian; I hope you understand why. He would have been shot immediately. Well, since they mistook him for a German, they cured him. But when he was discharged, he had nowhere to go since he did not live in Germany. And he also had no legs. His legs were amputated after the explosion that wounded him."

"What?" asked Martha. "He lost his legs?"

"Yes," replied Pawel.

"Oh my gosh, and what did he do? Where did he go then, and how did he move?" asked Martha.

"Then, Berta came to his aid. He had to lie to her. He first said that his entire family was dead and that he had nowhere to return to. She said, 'You can live with me. If you agree, I have a small house on the outskirts of the city.'

"Of course, he accepted her offer. He had no other choice. He could not tell her that he was Russian. He did not know how she would react to this. He thought that, when the Russians conquered this city, he would go to them and tell them exactly what had happened to him. But the Russian troops passed through this city very quickly, and he had no opportunity to meet them. Then, he thought the war would end soon, and then he would ask Berta to help him find the Russians and return to his homeland.

"Berta was a very friendly woman. She felt sorry for him. She took care of him every day as if he were her husband. They told her neighbors that Petro was her husband since there were a lot of curious people in the area. Month after month passed, and Berta fell in love with him. She asked, 'What if we really got married?' She thought he had no home and no relatives, and he had no legs. What would he do alone? Where would he go?

"She did not know about his plans then. She did not know that he was hoping to meet the Russians. Another month passed, and Petro thought, *If I return to Russia, it would only be abuse for my family.* He thought that it would be very difficult for Anna to have two children and a disabled husband.

"Petro decided he didn't know how she was going to take it, and he didn't want to be a burden to his family. Berta had no family, and she did not mind taking care of him. She had fallen in love with him. . . .

"For Petro, it was very difficult to reciprocate her feelings since he loved Anna. But over time, he saw that Berta really loved him. He had a sense of respect for her at first. Probably because Berta turned out to be a very extraordinary woman.

She had sacrificed so much so that he could live as comfortably as possible, and despite everything, she was always by his side.

"A year passed, and Petro decided to tell her the whole truth. He was no longer afraid of what would happen to him. If she informed on him that he was Russian, they would send him out of the country, and he would return home. He was still hoping.

"On May 9, 1946, one year after the end of the war with Germany, he finally decided to tell the whole truth to Berta. He told me all the details of the conversation. He said that he wanted to talk to her about it seriously. He said that, when he was found wounded, for some reason, a German hospital had accommodated him. But he was not German; he was Russian. But he had worked as a German teacher at school, so he knew German very well.

"He said to Berta, 'I apologize for lying to you. I feel guilty. Forgive me.' He asked her for forgiveness. Berta said, 'I found you wounded and changed your Russian clothes for German clothes. I took them off the dead German lying next to you. I could not leave you to die in the street, injured. I am a nurse, and my job is to help the wounded and sick, which I did.'

"My father was amazed by her story. That was why she had offered to let him live with her. She knew that he had no one in Germany. My father told her, 'Thank you for saving me from death, and thank you so much for everything you've done for me.'

"After this conversation, he changed his behavior toward Berta. He began to feel grateful to her, and gradually, it turned into more serious feelings. He proposed to marry her. Of course, she agreed. She had been waiting for this for a long time.

"But he didn't tell her one secret. He didn't tell her that he was married and that he had two children. War, as you know, changes the life path of many people. That's exactly what happened to my father. The war destroyed him, separated him from his wife and children in Russia. The war made him fall in love with the woman who saved his life."

Martha said, "And today, the war between Russia and Ukraine has brought our families together. Once again, the war has affected our lives. But now we know everything that happened to our grandfather. I think that this is just a miracle that happened to him. That he became alive thanks to Berta. It was she who saved the life of our grandfather, and she gave life to you. Now we've met, and it turns out that we have relatives here in Germany. An amazing life story."

Viktor joined the conversation: "I want to meet all my relatives. Let's make a family holiday on May 9 since our grandfather confessed and told the whole truth on this day. We will call our family holiday 'Truth Day.' On this day, we will all confess our secrets, and in doing so, we will help each other if necessary."

"But if someone needs help urgently," Leo said, "I suggest asking for help without waiting for May 9."

"So, where are we all going to meet?" asked Martha.

Pawel said, "I propose to do it at my house. Let's get together on Saturday night and spend two days together. We have enough rooms for everyone."

They agreed to meet, and after that, Leo and Pawel talked for a long time away from everyone. Martha did not pay much attention to this; she drank tea with Viktor and Ella.

Leo had arranged with Pawel that he would propose to Martha at his home. They discussed all the details.

Pawel said, "You should come to us and discuss everything. It will be better if everyone is ready for it except Martha. And I propose to do the wedding on May 9, in honor of my father and her grandfather. And her grandmother, I hope, won't be offended by him after what happened to him."

"I think she won't be offended by him after everything she's learned."

"And Berta won't mind it, as it's the family's Day of Truth. We will keep this tradition alive for our ancestors for many years to come," added Pawel.

They discussed all the details of the family acquaintance, and then Viktor and Ella drove Pawel back home.

Chapter 6
Birth of a New Family

On the appointed day, all the relatives came to Pawel's house, all the relatives on Pawel's side and all the relatives on Martha's side.

Before dinner, Pawel said, "I'd love to invite everyone to the hall, where I will introduce all the relatives from my side."

Everyone followed him. He had already discussed how he would do it. All the relatives lined up in order, a chain that made it very easy to explain who the next person was and how he was related to them.

Pawel began pointing to the portraits and said, "This is my father. His name is Petro."

Martha looked at her grandfather. She did not remember how he looked since her grandmother and mother had not shown her his photo.

He had huge brown eyes and dark hair. In the portrait, there were two dimples on both cheeks and a smile on his lips.

"And this," she heard, "is my mother. Her name is Berta."

Martha thought, *Thank you, Berta. You saved my grandfather from death.* Still, she caught herself thinking, *The woman who separated my grandmother from her husband.* "Yes," she said aloud. "Due to the unexpected situation, we now have relatives in Germany."

"Yes," Pawel agreed. "This is me, and this is my wife, Clara. Tragically, she died nine years ago."

Martha began to look at his wife's face. She was very pretty, with blue eyes, almost completely white hair, and a very friendly expression on her face.

She must have been a very affectionate mother to her children, Martha thought.

"And these," continued Pawel, "are our children." He pointed to those present. "This is my eldest son, Daniel. This is my daughter, Anna, and this is my youngest son, Henry."

Martha recognized the young man who had brought the letter; it was Henry.

She turned around and said, "It is a pleasure to meet you. My name is Martha. This is my brother, Viktor, and this is my fiancé, Leo."

"Well, that's fine," said Pawel. "Now we know each other, and if anyone has any questions, you can ask. But not now, after dinner," he added. "Sorry, I'm hungry; I'm always a little hungry when I'm worried. So, we'll have dinner first, and then we'll have a good conversation?"

"Yes," they replied in near unison.

"Well, let's all go to the dining room."

Martha entered the dining room; it was huge. There was a table in the middle. *And this table can hold about twenty people*, she thought.

Pawel put the names in their places, indicating who would sit where. For some reason, Martha and Leo were placed at the very end of the table. She noticed it but said nothing. *This is his house, and let everything be according to his rules*, she thought.

They sat down at the table.

Pawel said, "Before we start our first family dinner, Leo, would you like to say something?"

Everyone looked at Leo.

He stood up and pushed his chair as far away from the table as possible, as if he didn't have enough space.

Martha smiled. *How strange he is being today*, she thought.

Then, Leo began his speech: "Good evening. I am very glad that a new family has gathered in this house today, one that was formed and united after many years of separation. But I think that another family will be formed today, and I will be very happy if this happens."

He dropped to one knee and took out of his pocket the box containing his mother's wedding ring. He looked at Martha and said, "My beloved Martha, I ask for your hand and heart. Will you marry me?" he asked.

Martha was shocked. She had not expected such a turn of events. She looked at him and said nothing.

Leo asked again, "Are you going to be my wife?"

Martha seemed to wake up from a trance, realizing what was happening. She stood up, and Leo rose to his feet as well. He handed her the ring, took her hand, and put it on her finger.

"Martha, is that a yes?" he asked.

"Yes," replied Martha.

Everyone clapped their hands together, and Martha was still in shock.

Leo hugged her and kissed her. "I love you, I love you," he whispered in her ear.

"I love you too," she replied.

"Well, that's fabulous. Another family has formed here in this house. We have a happy home. Many families have been formed in it, and everyone has been happy over the years," said Pawel.

Martha asked, "Is this the house where my grandfather lived with Berta?"

"Yes," replied Pawel. "And then me and Clara and our children. This house belonged to Berta's parents. For many years, it belonged to her father, grandfather, great-grandfather. This house warmed a lot of family and their relatives."

He continued, "I am very proud of our ancestors. They were proper Germans. They did not fight in the war. They worked on their land and grew vegetables for others. They were farmers from generation to generation. Then, other farms appeared around us, more and more. But now, a city has grown up in this place.

"Our house ended up in this city, and it has survived to this day. Our house survived the Great Patriotic War. I am grateful to God for such a gift. Many families lost absolutely everything. We turned out to be lucky. Our home still warms our hearts."

"Wow," said Martha. "You really turned out to be lucky. But my parents died in the house, in our family home. Nothing remained of the house, not a single thing survived. Everything burned down or was destroyed by a bomb. Only Viktor turned out to be lucky; he survived."

Martha caught herself thinking that this was probably not the place for this discussion. "I'm sorry," she said. "Today, we have another reason to meet. Let's celebrate our happy moments."

Pawel proposed a toast. He stood up and said, "Let's drink to our family, to those who died, to those who survived, to those who now continue our family traditions. For our family, for our happy future. And finally, we will never forget our ancestors, who are not with us now. For them, for their memory, and for our successes in our continuing lives."

Everybody raised their wineglasses, stood up, and drank to the beautiful toast.

The dinner lasted a long time. Everyone ate and talked about the families that were now united into one big family, thanks to Petro and Berta and their historical survival.

Chapter 7
Wedding

The preparations for the wedding did not last long, as a large replenishment had taken place in Martha's family.

Martha, Margaret, Ella, Anna, Mary, and all the women were happy to take part in the organization of this special event.

It turned out that Mary was a qualified seamstress. She took Martha's measurements, showed her a drawing from a magazine, and in two weeks, the dress was ready.

Martha came to the last fitting, and of course, everyone participated in this, except for the men. Absolutely everyone was amazed by the beauty of the dress. Martha looked like a real princess. It was almost impossible to describe this dress. The style of the dress emphasized all the lines of her youthful and gorgeous-looking body.

Martha, for the first time in her life, was surprised that she admired her view in the mirror, looking again and again. She did not want to take off the dress.

Margaret said, "Well, it's time to shoot this beauty. Stop teasing us all, or we'll all want to get married."

Everyone was happy to spend all this time together. Between work, home, and wedding preparations, the women were busy twenty-four hours a day. But it brought them great pleasure.

Finally, the day came. Martha and all the women were in Martha's apartment. All the rest of the family and friends were at Pawel's house.

According to Ukrainian tradition, the groom had to come to the house of the bride with a ransom, which no one knew about, and the girlfriends had to come up with all the possible jokes on him they could. He had to overcome and go through all these trials and jokes.

When the groom's car turned into the street where Martha lived, all the friends in the car saw that the road was blocked by road signs. There was a huge sign in the middle, where it was written "STOP, REPAIRS ARE UNDERWAY DURING THE DAY."

Viktor said, "Here is the first obstacle for you."

"What am I supposed to do?" asked Leo.

Smiling, Viktor replied, "You're a groom; you have to find a way out of this situation."

Leo got out of the car, and he approached the two men standing near the sign.

"Good afternoon," he said. "Who decided to carry out this road repair on a Saturday?"

"This is our resolution," one of the men said and pulled out a huge sheet of paper. When unfolded, it turned into a long tablecloth, on which was written: "Close the road for Leo until he gives two glasses of vodka to those present."

After reading this, Leo laughed. "Okay!" He went back to the car, took out a bottle of vodka, and poured two shots.

The men drank and said, "Give us this bottle. We will deliver it to the right place."

"Of course," Leo agreed, and he laughed.

He poured them full glasses of vodka again, and they drank and removed the sign.

Leo's car drove up to the house where Martha lived, and they stopped near the entrance. Leo went to the door and tried to open it, but it wouldn't open.

"Well, here is the second obstacle," Viktor said aloud.

Leo asked loudly, "Who's behind the door? How much does the key with which I will open this door cost?"

There was a voice behind the door, and it answered, "Twenty dollars."

He pulled out twenty dollars and shoved it under the door. The door opened. Standing there were two women who lived in this building. They were Martha's neighbors.

Leo and his friends went up to the floor where Martha lived, and he rang the doorbell.

The door opened, and Mary and Margaret stood on the threshold. Margaret said, "Dear groom, we won't give you the bride until you dance for us," and they turned on the music.

Leo looked at Margaret and said, "Margaret, you know I can't dance."

Margaret laughed. "Don't you think I came up with this ransom because I found out that you don't know how to dance?" She laughed loudly and sang, "Come on, fiancé, dear, dance for us. Squat down like the Ukrainian Cossacks' dance."

Leo looked at them and said, "Well, I'm going to surprise you now, and let's dance in a crouch." He saw and knew how the Ukrainian folk dance was danced. He was very observant and talented, and he chose his own folk dance. "It's called 'Give Me My Fiancé.'"

Everyone began to clap their hands, supporting him.

"OMG," Martha said as she watched him.

At last, Leo came to Martha. He held out his hand to her and said, "Here's my hand for you. You already won my heart years ago."

Martha took his arm, and they went downstairs to the car. All the cars were dressed up in the Ukrainian style.

He put Martha in the car, and they drove to Pawel's house. When they reached Pawel's house, they saw many dressed up cars. Leo kept his eyes on Martha, and Martha was happy. She radiated a tremendous amount of light, joy, and happiness. Leo was happy to see her in this state.

Their eyes met, and they both froze for a moment from these feelings. In this very moment, they both realized that this was exactly what they were missing in their lives—belonging to each other.

They didn't say anything; they just looked at each other. And they were in the same happy atmosphere, which they had both dreamed of for a long time.

"I love you," said Leo.

"I love you too," replied Martha.

They entered the house, where everything was ready for their wedding. The ceremony was held in a solemn atmosphere. There was not a single person in the house who did not feel happy on this day.

Two people named Leo and Martha were the happiest on our planet.

After the betrothal ceremony, everyone was invited to the hall. Ukrainian German dishes were cooked for dinner.

Everyone was satisfied from tasting various dishes and, of course, from the wine and brandy.

Leo whispered in Martha's ear, "The honeymoon will start now. Follow me."

He went into the dining room, and Pawel showed him a new way out of the house. Martha followed him, and as soon as they stepped outside, grains of wheat and rose petals fell on them from all sides. Martha and Leo saw a car that was parked near the house. They ran to it very quickly, got in, and drove to meet their happy, married life.

They spent their honeymoon in Germany in a somewhat small town in the house where Leo's parents' family once lived. This was his family heritage. He'd always loved this house and didn't want to sell it, so he had rented it out year after year. The house had been vacant for a few months, so he had decided to spend the honeymoon month in the house of his ancestors.

He planned to tell Martha about his family and about his childhood and young years spent in this house.

Chapter 8
Honeymoon

Martha did not know where they were going; it was a surprise for her. But she was pleasantly surprised when the car drove into the courtyard of the estate. There was a very beautifully decorated greenhouse of flowers and shrubs. Not far from the house, there was a small lake, or rather, a pond.

Getting out of the car, Martha was amazed by the surrounding beauty of the house and the site.

"OMG," she said. "What an unforgettable honeymoon. I really like it here. How did you find such beauty?"

Leo said, "For you, dear, I will find anything you want and at any time of the day or night." He hugged her tightly and kissed her. "We are at home."

"Okay," Martha answered. "For how many days did you rent this house?"

Leo said, "This is my house. This house has belonged to our family for over two hundred years."

"What?" wondered Martha. "Do you mean it's all yours?"

"Yes, all this is ours. I inherited this house. I used to rent out. Now we must think about what we are going to do with it."

Martha replied without hesitation, "We will live here and raise our children and grandchildren." Then, she hugged her husband.

He took her in his arms, and they disappeared behind the door of their new residence.

The house most looked like a small castle. It had three floors. On the first floor, there was a kitchen, a dining room for workers, a dining room for the family, and a dining room for holidays. Such a dining room could accommodate forty people without any problems.

There were fifteen chairs on one side of the table, fifteen chairs on the other side, and ten chairs in the middle, but if desired, it was possible to add more since the chairs stood far from each other.

On the first floor, there was also a waiting room for receptions and for unexpected guests. Since Leo's father had also been a doctor, he often had unexpected guests. There was a small clinic for them to give first aid to the patients.

On the second floor, the family lived on one side, and on the other side were rooms for their guests. In the area where the family lived, there were five rooms, one of which was a master bedroom.

On the third floor lived people who worked in the house and on the estate, taking care of everything that surrounded the house, including the pond.

Martha didn't know any of this yet. She could not have imagined that she would live in a palace.

The family was very famous in Germany, prosperous and successful in the organization of the polyclinic from generation to generation. The profession of doctor was passed on with respect and laden with very serious relationships with patients.

Both at home and during the war, they had organized a hospital and helped the wounded, not only from the German side. They had not chosen among the wounded, just helped everyone they found and those who came to them.

Leo was proud of his family and always told the stories he knew. He knew many of them, but he had never told Martha about them. He had explained that he was afraid that she might take it as boasting on his part. Now he would have to tell the whole truth.

In a small medical office, there were photos on the wall. They had been taken before the war, during the war, and after the war. When Leo's grandfather and father had lived in this house, the clinic was open to everyone.

The next morning, there was a knock on the room where Martha and Leo were sleeping.

"Who is it?" she asked with amazement in her voice.

"Don't worry; it's probably a housekeeper. I think she's wondering if we'll have breakfast or not," he replied.

"What?" she asked again. "You have a housekeeper?"

"Yes," Leo replied. "I don't live here, and she makes sure everything is in order. You like the area around the house and the pond, don't you? So who do you think looks after it?"

"Yes," agreed Martha, still not believing that she had married a man who had worked as a surgeon on the front line in Ukraine. And now he had also turned out to be a very prosperous man. He had his own employees who served him.

Yes, she thought, *I didn't have a family until last night, and here, this morning, I suspect we'll have a family.*

Leo got out of bed and went out. He left the room and was gone for a few minutes.

When he returned, he said, "She has organized breakfast on the veranda. It's very convenient for two. Very nice view of the surrounding homestead. I hope you like it?"

They went down to the veranda an hour later. Only now did Martha look around, and she was stunned by what she saw.

The house really looked like a small palace. It was like an old German palace, with all the amenities and furnishings, in the style of the old German society.

"Wow!" she said aloud as she walked past all the rooms on the right and left sides. "OMG, how many rooms are there in this house?"

Leo turned to her and said, "At first, it seems there's like a lot of them, but when you live here for a month, everything will seem small and cozy."

They came out onto the veranda. It was comfortable and very convenient for two. *It's a place of solitude*, she thought.

After breakfast, Leo showed her the first floor. He decided that it would be enough for her on the first day because Martha was already very upset and not happy that they had such a huge estate. He did not know how she felt and was afraid that she would not want to stay in this house.

Martha felt uncomfortable in this house, probably because the house where she grew up had been small. It had had only one floor, three bedrooms, a kitchen, and a hall. She loved her home and her room. It had been comfortable for her, and there, she had spent her happy childhood and youth. This house was huge, and so far, she did not feel cozy, comfortable, and warm in it. Her husband saw this and tried to help her improve her opinion of this house. He created all possible conveniences for her.

He thought, *Then we will just come here for weekends and vacations.* Leo loved his home and did not plan to part with it in any way, under any circumstances.

They spent two weeks in the house. Martha began to get used to the fact that she didn't have to cook breakfast. She hadn't seen the kitchen at all for two weeks.

They walked around the estate, swam, and sunbathed near the pond. And of course, they began to run, as they had both begun to gain weight. Morning exercises became normal for them. Martha didn't want to be bigger than she was now.

"Only 120," she said, "and no pound more." She adhered to the routine very seriously.

Leo also treated his weight and health very seriously. He said, "I remember my grandfather once said, 'A doctor must look younger than his age and have an athletic body and build, and only then will patients believe everything he advises them.' If you are fat and have problems with your health, you think that patients will believe you? 'Since you can't even help yourself, how can you help me?' Every patient will have this question. He adhered to this rule very clearly. It could be said to be the law of his life."

Martha stuck to it too. Well, sometimes. She allowed herself to relax a little. She didn't eat much, but she just loved tea and very tasty pastries. This was probably because she had been born in Ukraine. Tea and homemade pastries were in every home, without exception. She could easily replace her lunch or dinner with just a cup of tea and a bun of jam or, of course, butter. She could not imagine life without these three products. She didn't gain weight; she always stayed 120 pounds.

One morning, at breakfast, Leo asked, "Do we need to discuss where and when we will live?"

"What do you suggest?" Martha asked.

Leo replied, "I would like to live here, permanently. I am not far from my job. Only thirty-five minutes' drive. What do you think?"

Martha's reply surprised him. "I agree," she said, "but I would like to go to college. I want to become a surgeon." She looked at Leo and waited for his answer.

Leo looked at her and thought. After a moment, he replied, "I don't mind if you want to become a surgeon. Here is just one question: what do you think about children? I remember you said we were going to have a lot of children. If we have a lot of children, I don't think it's a good idea to be a surgeon. I think that the children would like to have and be together with their mother. I understand that we will have a nanny. But I don't want the kids to see their mom one hour a day." He paused. Then, he added, "It's just my reflection. If you want, we can wait with the children." He looked at Martha.

Martha replied, "I'll be honest; I don't know. Let's think a little more about what we're going to do."

"Okay, I'm going to work next Monday. We will return to the city. Let's live in the city, and you talk to your brother. You will live with him in our house in the city. You have two more weeks of vacation."

"I think this will lead to making the right decision. I should go home and discuss everything with Viktor. And live at home with you in your house," she added.

"In our house," Leo corrected.

Martha smiled and replied, "Yes, in our house."

She rested her head on his shoulder, and they sat in such an embrace, looking at the charm of the nature around them.

Chapter 9
Return to the City

Returning to the city, Martha said, "I have to go to visit Viktor."

"Of course," Leo replied.

Martha called Viktor and let him know that she was coming to visit him.

Viktor was happy. "I miss you. I don't want to live without you for so long." He suddenly fell silent.

"What's wrong?" asked Martha.

"It's okay. We'll talk when you arrive."

Martha thought he must have had a quarrel with Ella. She told Leo and said, "I have to go see him and talk."

"Do you want me to go with you?" he asked.

"No, I will be okay," said Martha. "He will be honest if only I come."

She kissed her husband and left the house. She went to her apartment quickly and opened the door with her key. When she entered, she saw that Viktor was sitting on the sofa alone, reading a book.

He's reading a book, so he can concentrate. That's good. Probably nothing bad has happened, she hoped in her heart.

When he heard Martha enter, Viktor immediately stood up and rushed to meet her. He embraced her, and resting his head on her shoulder, he cried.

Martha asked him to sit on the sofa and sat down next to him, hugging him around his shoulders. He lowered his head onto her lap. He had always done this with their mother in those distant days when they had lived in Ukraine and she had been alive.

Martha began to stroke his head. She remembered how her mother had calmed him.

But he was just a boy then, thought Martha. *And now he is an adult man. The war and all the circumstances forced him to grow up very quickly. What happened?* She was dying to guess, but she decided she would not force him to talk. *I will wait until he calms down and tells me everything he considers necessary.* Martha continued to sit and stroke his head and back.

Viktor finally calmed down. He sat down, and looking into his sister's eyes, he said, "I'm sorry that I've become so unstable in my feelings."

Martha said, "Viktor, there's nothing wrong with crying or talking about your feelings. Share with a loved one. This is the most normal setting for discussing any issue. Yesterday, me and Leo also discussed our problems and how to solve them. Everyone has a loved one for such moments."

Viktor said, "Do you have problems with Leo?" He was worried.

"No," replied Martha. "This is not a family problem. This is a matter that we should discuss together and make a decision about that suits both of us. Compromise, roundtable talks," she added, smiling, trying to cheer her brother up. "The two parties are negotiating amicably and discussing details for the future," said Martha, laughing.

Viktor smiled slightly. "Thank you, sis. What would I do without you? Martha, do you remember that I told you Ella and I are getting married and that we will have many children?"

"Yes, of course. I remember it very well," replied Martha.

"A week ago, Ella felt pain in her stomach. I immediately called the ambulance and her father. Her father arrived faster than the ambulance. Patrick examined her, and when the ambulance arrived, they gave her painkillers, and Patrick said, 'I would like to take her to my hospital.' They took her to her father's hospital. Patrick examined her and found that she had a tumor in her uterus. They did an urgent operation. They had to remove the entire uterus because the tumor was huge. He said that removing the uterus would be much easier than doing all the possible procedures. It would be safer. He explained to me that it would be better and the tumor would not return. They did all kinds of tests. The good news is that this is not cancer. The bad news is that we will not have children."

Martha asked, "Viktor, did you and Ella have sexual relations?"

"Yes," Viktor replied. "She was with me all this time when you went to Leo's."

"And how does Patrick feel about this?"

"He talked to me. I explained to him that I plan to propose to her as soon as you and Leo come back. She's in the hospital right now under his care."

"At what time can we visit her?"

"Anytime," Viktor replied. "Everyone knows that this is Patrick's daughter and that I am your brother."

"Then get ready. We'll go visit her now."

Viktor quickly pulled himself together.

"We'll go in my car," Martha suggested. "I'll come home here anyway."

"Home?" repeated Viktor. "You have another home now," he added, smiling.

"Yes, I will live with Leo, and this apartment will be yours and Ella's. If you have no other plans?" asked Martha. "Patrick has a big house. Maybe Ella would like to live at home?"

"No," replied Viktor. "We have already talked about this topic. We will live here on our own, regardless of what our parents think. That's what Ella wants."

"I like her decision. She is a very smart girl. A family is a family. You must start from scratch. You must live together. Achieve everything yourself. Thus, the family will be strong for many years. Your home, your homeland, your shared traditions and rules," Martha mused aloud.

"Wow, she said about the same thing," Viktor replied.

Soon, they arrived at the hospital where Martha, her husband, and Patrick worked. And where Ella, Viktor's future wife, was currently located.

Upon entering the surgical ward, Martha saw Leo. He was having a conversation with his friend Patrick. Martha and Viktor approached them.

"Hello, Patrick," said Martha.

"Hello," said Viktor.

"Welcome back," Patrick said and held out his hand to Martha.

"Thank you," she replied.

Martha looked around. She missed her work. She realized that she did not want to live in the country. She wanted to study to be a surgeon, to work here with her husband and Patrick. She didn't say anything to her husband, but she was glad to be back at the hospital. She couldn't wait for her return to the operating room. *I'm not made to be a 50 percent mom. If I am a mother, I will be at home with the children every minute of their lives. I want us to grow up together. They grow up, and I get old, but I want it to happen together,* Martha thought. *I understand now that I must be here in the hospital to help the sick; that's what I really feel now.*

Martha also felt and realized that she could not live in a house outside the city. *How will I explain it to him?* she thought.

Patrick said, "Let's go see Ella. I think she's awake."

They all went together to the ward where Ella was lying.

Leo took Martha's hand and pulled it, as if pausing. Martha realized that he had seen her expression when they had arrived at the hospital. He had realized that she missed her job.

"You are silent this morning. What happened?" he asked.

"Yes," said Martha in surprise. "Viktor cried when I returned home. I can't leave him in such a moment, in such a state. Now I must be next to him until Ella returns. Viktor said that he plans to propose to Ella."

"Yes?" said Leo. "This would make a great positive impact on her physical condition after surgery."

"Yes, I think so too," replied Martha.

Entering the room, Viktor very quickly ran up to Ella. She smiled when she saw everyone who had come. Viktor hugged her and kissed her. Martha came up, took her hand, and kissed her on the cheek.

As Ella's attending physicians, Leo and her father were serious, but at the same time, they were very worried about Ella's health.

"Martha, where did you go on your secluded honeymoon?" Ella asked.

With a smile, Martha replied, "You won't believe it. Leo has a house outside the city. He was born and raised there. This manor house has belonged to his family for two hundred years or even more."

"256 years," Leo specified.

Martha continued, "It's a very nice house, with old architecture that looks like new. The estate is cared for by people who live in this house. They do not leave. It's passed down from generation to generation."

"Maybe a few dozen people now," Leo added.

"A few dozen?" asked Ella.

"According to you, Martha, it looks like a palace."

Martha smiled and replied, "Yes, I said so too when I saw the house. It's not a house; it's a palace."

"Leo, are you rich? And you work in the hospital?" asked Ella.

"Yes," he replied. "All my ancestors were doctors. I walked in their footsteps. As for being rich, I'm not that rich. I just inherited this house from my parents. They received it from their parents, so this has accumulated over the years. Now I must take care of all of it since it is the past of my ancestors. There's no way I can let down their hopes for me."

"Of course," Ella replied.

Ella recovered quickly and, after talking to Viktor, suggested that everyone go to Leo's house. Since Viktor would be proposing to Ella, this was a suitable place, perfect for such a celebration.

From there, Martha and Leo went to work without any problems.

Viktor rested with Ella after the operation on his girlfriend and future bride and wife.

That night, there would be a family dinner. The whole family would come from both Ella and Viktor's sides. Viktor also invited their new family from their grandfather's side.

Huge tables for guests were set up in the dining room, and all those present only occupied half of all the tables.

Dinner began with a toast, in which Leo said, "My dear relatives, I am so glad that a huge number of relatives have appeared in our house again. You can't imagine how glad I am that life has reappeared within these walls.

"This house has been empty for many years, and finally, here, it's not. Thank you all very much for being here. You know that the doors of this house are open to all of you at any time. Just let me and Martha know, and we will arrange everything you need for you, even transport. For now, I'd like to have this glass of wine for our growing family." He raised his glass, and everyone followed.

Dinner took place in a friendly, family atmosphere.

Suddenly, Viktor stood up and said, "I ask for a minute of attention."

Everyone fell silent and looked at him.

"As you all already know," Viktor said, "Ella and I have been dating for a long time. I think it's time to change our marital status. I don't want to be just Ella and Viktor. I want to be more."

He took a black box out of his pocket, opened it, and inside that box was his mother's ring, which his father had given her for their anniversary. There was a ruby in the center, and there were several small diamonds around it.

He knelt on one knee in front of Ella and said, "Ella, I have loved you since the minute I saw you. I already knew then that this ring would belong only to you. Dear Ella, will you be my wife?"

Ella cried, got up, and hugged Viktor. She answered, "Yes, I'll be your wife. I have no doubt that we will be together for the rest of our lives. I've known it since the moment we met."

Martha was glad that Viktor would not be alone now. He had a woman who would love him.

Viktor had once said to Martha, "Ella is my soulmate. We understand each other without saying a word."

Dinner was held in a solemn atmosphere. Everyone congratulated Ella and Viktor.

After dinner, Martha decided to talk to Ella alone. She invited her to the balcony, where there were only two chairs. She put Ella in one of them, and the other she took for herself. She began to tell her about how Leo and she sat there in the evenings and admired the beauty of the setting sun.

Then, she asked, "What are your plans? What are you going to do now after such a big change?"

Ella said, "I will take a leave of absence for one year from the institute. Viktor said that we must first arrange our life, my health, and our place of residence, bring everything to a stable environment."

"I'm thinking about it too," Martha told her. "I suggest you move here to live in this house. The house is large, and we have enough space. We are now one family. Here, you will be in the fresh air; you will have enough time to restore your health. You won't have to worry about what to cook for dinner or lunch, and you'll forget where the kitchen is. How I did it during my stay here is, in fact, very interesting, and I even like it. I am used to not cooking.

"I'm with Leo. We'll see you more often, and we'll be together. I think, if you want to be alone, it's possible in this house. We won't bother you, and vice versa. If me and

Leo are busy, that's also possible. This is my proposal, of course. I do not insist, but I would like to see you as often as possible. Of course, think about it. Discuss everything and let us know."

Martha looked at Ella. She smiled and continued, "I hope there will be a positive response. We'll be waiting to live here and in the city because I want to go to college. I want to study to be a surgeon, so you'll have plenty of time to miss us. But I would like our family to live in this house since this house belongs to my husband and me. I don't want it to be empty. We now have family members who can live here forever until the next generation."

Martha fell silent. She realized that she had made a mistake talking about the generations to be created since Ella could no longer have children after the operation.

She immediately corrected herself: "Ella, I suggest that you adopt a girl or a boy. Or maybe two at once. This way, you will have your own family. This surgery should not affect your life. It's just an operation, but let it happen. Life goes on; life doesn't stop there. Or you can find a woman who will carry your baby for nine months. It's now possible. Your egg and Viktor's sperm, and that's all you will need to have a child. It's so simple and easy these days." She fell silent again and looked at Ella.

"Yes, Viktor and I talked about this topic. Well, until we decided that I should take care of my health. Maybe in a year. We'll see," Ella answered.

"Yes, of course. You will be comfortable here. You can sit, sleep as much as you want, eat what you want, sunbathe, swim, and take long walks. Viktor will stay at home, and when he goes anywhere, you have Tarzan."

"Tarzan?" asked Ella. "Who is that?"

"We have a German shepherd here. His name is Tarzan. He loves to walk around the homestead. As soon as he sees someone walking, he immediately keeps them company."

Ella said, "We also had a dog, but it died, and after that, we decided that we would not have any more dogs. But I missed her for a very long time." She repeated the name. "Tarzan? I want to meet him."

"Let's go for a little walk tomorrow morning. To the pond. We can sit there, and Viktor and, of course, Tarzan will come with us," Martha suggested.

"I agree. This is exactly what I am missing. Just relaxing and gaining strength. Increasing the duration of my walk a little each time."

"Yes, I think so. It's a great idea."

Martha was glad that Ella had almost accepted her suggestion of living in a house with her and Leo.

Soon, Viktor entered the balcony. "Finally, I've found you," he said. "Are you hiding from me?"

Ella laughed. "We just found a cozy corner to relax."

Viktor looked around. "Yes, this is really a corner for relaxation and, as I understand it, is only for two." Looking around, he saw only two chairs.

"Yes, of course it's for two, and that's why I'm leaving and leaving you to watch the sunset. I've seen it many times before. Bye," Martha said.

She looked at two people happily in love. Her brother and her sister-in-law were happy and young. She was very happy about it. "Okay," she added, "I'll go get a room ready for you," and she walked out with a worried look.

As soon as she entered the living room, she saw Leo. He was walking toward her. "I've been looking for you all over the house. Where were you hiding from me?" he asked.

Martha laughed. "For some reason, everyone thinks I'm hiding. Me and Ella, we were sitting on the balcony. Now Ella and Viktor are there. I don't think we need to bother them," she added, smiling.

"Yes, of course," Leo agreed.

Martha asked, "Do you think the rooms are ready for our guests?"

"Of course. It's done. I took care of it before everyone arrived."

"Great," said Martha. "I hope you put Ella and Viktor next to us."

"They need a room near the stairs. Of course they'll be next to us," Leo replied.

Martha hugged her husband and said, "Leo, I did—" She choked on air for a moment because, for the first time, she had decided without consulting her husband. "Without consulting you, I offered to let Ella live here in our house. I know you'll be offended by me for this, but I think they're our family. I want to be with them."

Leo put his finger on her lips, as if stopping her next sentences. He looked at her and said, "My dear, this is our home, and I would be glad if Ella and Viktor lived here with us."

"Yay!" shouted Martha. "I was so afraid that you would mind."

"Why did you think that I would be against it? This house can accommodate a lot of people, and if you want to invite someone, there is no problem," he replied. "I want life to appear in this house again. Our whole family will live in this house for many years, from generation to generation. Our family tradition will continue."

"Thank you, dear," replied Martha.

She had not yet told him about her decision to go to college and sometimes live in the city. But she was glad that Viktor and Ella would live with them.

Their family was growing by leaps and bounds, and Martha was happy.

Chapter 10
University

After a few days of rest in the house, Martha showed Viktor and Ella almost the whole house.

She asked, "Which room would you like to live in? Outside the bedroom, I mean, since all the other rooms belong to all of us."

Viktor only smiled and answered, "I will be happy to live in any room of this house. After living in a small house in Ukraine and after our house was destroyed, I thought for a long time that I would be homeless. So now I am grateful to God that I have such a beautiful home and a new family. Let Ella make this decision. I will be happy to be with her in any room."

Ella made a questioning face, then she put her index finger to her cheek, as if imitating a playful posture and at the same time thinking about her decision. She replied, "I like the room where we live now."

"I knew it," Martha said. "Leo, he knows what he's doing. He's the one who chose the room for you. Fine, we must transport your things and everything you would like to have to your room. We can even change the scenery if you want."

"No," Ella replied. "Let everything remain as it is. We will only transport our clothes from our home."

"Okay," agreed Martha.

Viktor and his wife's relocation to a new place of residence, to a house outside the city which belonged to Martha and her husband, was very fast and successful. Martha moved back and forth between Leo's house in the city and, of course, the family home outside the city.

One evening, as they were both driving home after work, they decided to stay in town. On this day, a lot of wounded were brought from Ukraine. They were both very tired, and they ordered dinner. . . .

There was a very difficult situation on the front of Ukraine and Russia. From the state of the war, it could be understood that both sides were already tired of such long action. Ukrainians, including the president of Ukraine fought for their homeland like heroes. Russia's military forces were tired of being called murderers right to their faces. Many of them did not understand why this war existed.

It sounded like the Russians were killing Russians because they lived on the territory of the newly formed state called Ukraine. It was not clear why Russia accepted the new countries like Belarus, Latvia, Estonia, Kazakhstan, Uzbekistan, and so on but did not want to recognize Ukraine. An incomprehensible political question.

Every time Martha was in the operating room and there was a Ukrainian lying on the table, she thought about why it wasn't her mom or dad and why they had to die. But she served the doctor, helped do the operation, and, at the same time, prayed for the wounded person.

Leo and Martha had dinner, and they soon both fell asleep on the couch.

Martha woke up at about a quarter to two. She woke Leo up and said, "Dear, let's go to the bedroom."

They hugged and went to the bedroom. It was not long before morning, and they fell asleep again. But at seven o'clock, the phone rang.

Who could it be? Martha thought.

She picked up the phone and heard a voice on the other side. Someone was crying and talking very quickly, which was completely incomprehensible to Martha.

"Who is this?" she asked. "Calm down. Tell me what happened."

Martha finally realized that it was Viktor. She sat up on the bed. "What's wrong? Calm down. I don't understand anything you're saying."

Finally, Viktor gathered his strength and answered, "Ella has been taken to the hospital, and I am going to see her. . . ."

Martha stopped him. "Okay, go. I will talk to you when you're there. We'll meet you at the hospital."

She hung up, and Leo already realized what had happened. They quickly packed up, and in half an hour, they were already inside the hospital.

Ella had just been brought in; she was unconscious. Her father and Leo examined her but couldn't figure out what had happened to her.

They decided that it was necessary to perform surgery. They prepared the operating room and said to Martha, "Martha, you're not going to be in the operating room. You're going to stay with Viktor."

At first, Martha wanted to object, but then, after looking at her brother, she realized that it would be better and decided to stay with him.

Viktor was horrified by what had happened. He said that everything had been fine until the evening. "We went to the bedroom. Suddenly, Ella said that she was nauseous. She turned pale and ran to the toilet, and of course, I followed her. She said she didn't want me to see her like that and asked me to go out.

"I went out, standing outside the door, and I listened to her vomiting. After a few moments, everything became quiet. I thought, *Good, maybe she is just tired of moving, or maybe she ate something that did not suit her.*

"I asked how she was feeling. But there was no answer, and then, I could not stand it anymore and opened the door. She was lying on the floor. Her face was like a white marble wall. I was trying to wake her up. I shook her with all my might, but she did not wake up. There was no kind of life in her. I felt her pulse. The pulse was very weak, so I called Patrick and an ambulance. Then, I dialed you when the ambulance was already out of the house."

Martha hugged her brother and stroked his back. "It's okay. Everything will be fine. There are two of the best surgeons in the operating room. They will do anything to save Ella," she reassured.

The operation did not last long. Leo came out first. From his face, you could tell that something was wrong. Martha knew from his face that Ella had died on the operating table.

Patrick, her father, was still with her. He didn't come out. He could not believe that he could not save his own daughter from death. But they had done everything they could. The heart had just stopped, and no matter what they had done, it wouldn't work.

Viktor looked at Martha. For the second time in her life, Martha did not know what to do, what to say. She had had the same feeling when she saw her parents lying outside on a stretcher, covered with white sheets.

Leo walked up to Viktor. He hugged him and said, "I'm so sorry, but we couldn't do anything. We did absolutely everything possible and impossible. But we unfortunately could not save her."

Viktor began to beat his hands on Leo's chest and cry so loudly that everyone around him realized the bad outcome of the operation.

Martha decided to go to Patrick's aid. Entering the operating room, she saw Patrick sitting next to Ella, his hand resting on his daughter's head. He raised his eyes to Martha, and looking at her without saying anything, he got up and went to meet her.

He walked over to Martha, looked her straight in the eye, and whispered, "This is my last surgery. I won't be operating after this. I couldn't save my daughter. I couldn't save my daughter. Do you understand? What does that mean?"

"We'll talk about that later," Martha said. "But now, we need to get the whole family together, not here in the hospital but in our home."

"Yes," Patrick agreed. "I don't know how I'm going to tell my wife about it. She'll never forgive me for this."

"What are you talking about? She won't say a word. It's not your fault. It's a special case, and sometimes, we just can't do anything."

Patrick didn't answer. He just sat next to his daughter, holding her hand. Martha was powerless to say or do anything to reduce his pain. She caught herself thinking that she, too, was in the same state as Patrick. She just couldn't change anything, do anything, in a hopeless situation.

She brought Viktor into the operating room. Martha looked at her brother and thought, *Nothing can help people at this moment. They must realize for themselves what has happened and accept this loss. And all the talk will only cause slower healing of the grief from their loss. Those who find themselves in such a situation need time and, of course, people next to them to give them love and support.*

The funeral took place in the family cemetery, which was located on the homestead of Patrick and Mary's home.

There were only six people there: their great-grandparents, their grandparents, and Patrick's father and mother. For the first time, they buried their daughter before her parents.

The pain was certainly indescribable, but each of those present experienced this loss on their own, with their own thoughts and feelings. This was a strange and unexpected disaster.

Silence knocked on the door and for a long time.

Patrick did retire. He said, "I can't do surgery after I lost my daughter on the operating table. On my operating table."

Mary and Patrick went to their daughter's grave every morning and every evening. Martha found out after Margaret called her.

"We must take them somewhere," Margaret suggested. "Otherwise, they will be suffering from this loss for a long time. They need something to distract them."

"What if we invite them to our home?" Martha asked. "For the weekend. Let's say Viktor needs their support."

"Good idea," Margaret agreed. "I'll go right away and talk to them, tell them that you called and what you want. That you're very concerned about Viktor. I know they won't be able to refuse to help Viktor."

"Fine. I'm sorry, but I must warn Viktor about everything so that he is ready for their arrival. We need to make them believe us," Martha added.

"I'll let you know," Margaret replied.

Margaret called about an hour later. "Well, when are you coming?" asked Martha.

"Yes, we'll be at your house tomorrow, somewhere around noon."

"See you tomorrow," Martha replied.

She had already warned Viktor about the behavior of Patrick and Mary and that they would come tomorrow.

Before they went to Leo's house, Patrick and Mary visited their daughter's grave. Patrick, as always, sat down on a bench near her grave. Mary sat down beside him. He embraced her, and they sat silently, as if listening to what their daughter was saying. Each of them, of course, composed their own conversation. Patrick apologized to his daughter for not being able to save her from death. He felt guilty that she had died on his operating table. He said to her in his mind, *I will never forgive myself for this.* Mary told her daughter that Leo and Martha had invited them to visit and that they would see Viktor. She promised her that she would send him greetings from her. Then, she noticed how scary "I will say hello from you," sounded. *I will not be able to do this since you are no longer with us,* she thought. *I miss you terribly. And I*

don't want to believe that I won't see you again, neither in the morning when everyone eats breakfast nor in the evening after school. Where are you, my daughter? What happened? Why did you leave us? And she began to cry.

Patrick said, "Let's go. We're already late. We promised to be there after noon, and the time is already 1 p.m."

He got up from the bench, gave his hand to his wife, and helped her up, and after he put his arm around her shoulders, they walked toward the house.

They drove out of the house. The road led through the huge gate of their homestead. They were in no hurry, for they knew that they would see Viktor. He would also remind them of the death of their daughter.

Patrick said, "Wherever we go, wherever we go, everything reminds us of her. It will never cease to be so. We just need to get used to this pain and remember it in our hearts and minds. Without giving a show to others."

Mary began to cry again after this statement from Patrick. They drove in silence for Leo and Marta's house.

Leo and Martha and Viktor were sitting on the veranda, waiting for guests. It was approaching about one o'clock in the afternoon, but their guests were still not there.

"I think they're just not in a hurry at the moment," Martha said to reassure everyone. "In this case, everything's in slow motion."

Viktor stood up and said, "I'm very worried. I think I need to take a sedative. This is the first time I'll see them since the funeral. For some reason, I think they don't want to see me because I remind them of a terrible day here."

"What do you have to do with it? You had nothing to do with it. You didn't hurt her at all. On the contrary, you tried to help her as much as you could.

"It's just fate," Leo said. "No one knows where or when we're going to leave this world." On Leo's face was written what he was thinking about now.

Martha asked, "Honey, what are you talking about? What's wrong with your health? What are you talking about?"

"No, it's okay. It's not with me. I just thought about how it is, how scary a person's life is and how one second changes everything. Everything is gone. How scary it is for the people around you."

"Yes," Viktor replied. "All our plans collapsed without warning. I would never have thought this could happen. We were healthy and happy. What happened?"

"Only God knows what happened," Leo finished.

Chapter 11
Unexpected Acquaintances

Work, study, and life went on as if nothing had happened. Life goes on regardless of what happens to you, no matter how you feel. Sometimes, you feel like your life has stopped, but trust me, nothing can stop your life.

Even after such words as "My wife died, and my life died with her," life goes on anyway. It's time you survive and get used to the loss and the pain you've endured.

Viktor thought about his wife very often. He remembered their happy moments of life. He tried to forget that terrible day, but he couldn't forget it. He just knew it had happened and he couldn't change it. He was used to a new life without his wife.

One day, his beloved new friend and relative Henry invited him to dinner, where he would meet Henry's friends. Henry said that he would pick him up since it was a new restaurant and he himself did not know exactly where it was located. He jokingly remarked, "We'll investigate together."

Henry called Viktor from the car. "Hello, I'm here, near the house. Come out."

"Okay," replied Viktor.

He wrote a note for Martha about where he was and when he would return. As he stepped outside, he searched for Henry's car. Suddenly, he saw Henry waving to him.

Viktor went to meet him, and when he approached the car, he saw that a girl was sitting inside. She smiled, looking at him. Viktor got into the car and greeted them. His first question was, "In what language will we be talking?" He was used to speaking Russian with Henry.

Henry laughed. "In Russian," he replied.

"Okay?" asked Viktor in surprise.

"Yes," said the girl, looking at him again and smiling.

Then, Viktor stretched out his hand to her and introduced himself: "My name is Viktor, and yours?"

"My name is Zhenia," she replied and shook his hand.

"Zhenia," Viktor repeated. "A beautiful name."

Henry said, "She's just arrived, or rather, moved from Russia."

"From Russia?" asked Viktor again.

"Yes," the girl said, entering the conversation again. "My husband was sent to the war with Ukraine. He refused. They wanted to put him in prison for betraying the Motherland. He ran away somewhere. I still don't know where he is. I urgently moved to Germany through the German embassy since I was also threatened with prison. They think that I was hiding him. But I don't really know where he is."

"That is a story," Viktor said aloud. "I hope he will be found soon."

But for some reason, Viktor had the idea that he was probably no longer alive. In Russia, refusing to go to war had a deadly punishment. But he said nothing. It was clear that his wife was not discouraged. Viktor hoped to meet her husband.

They found a restaurant without too much difficulty. It was a restaurant called Gorreshpt.

When they stopped in the parking lot near the restaurant, Viktor got out of the car, and he, as always, was a gentleman. He went to the door where Zhenia was sitting and opened the car door for her.

"Wow, gentlemen haven't died out yet," she said aloud. "My husband is also a gentleman. He always knows how to take care of a woman."

Zhenia took Viktor by the arm, and all three of them went in the direction of the restaurant.

Once inside, they said that they were meeting with friends, and the host immediately led them to a table where several people were sitting. This was Viktor's first meeting with friends after Ella's death.

Viktor felt a little guilty, but he thought, if Ella were alive, she wouldn't mind that he had finally left the house for something other than work or study. *I know that she would approve of my decision. I must start communicating with people. This is my profession; this is my life.* No, he thought, *this is a necessity for every person.* He had to communicate with friends and just live regardless of any circumstances. *That's what our life has given to us.* Then, for some reason, he thought, *Every ending brings new beginnings. Yes, I will never forget Ella, but I must live.*

They sat down at a table, and Henry introduced his friends to everyone present.

Viktor asked again, "What language are we going to speak?"

Zhenia replied, "German. I don't like to create an uncomfortable environment for the waiters and all the people around us."

"Well said," added Henry.

They ordered dinner, ate, and talked about work, study, and new books they had read. Viktor finally felt like a normal person.

The evening turned out to be magnificent.

As they drove home, Henry said to Viktor, "I'll take Zhenia home first because it's on the way and then you, okay?"

"Yes, of course. Do as you like."

They drove Zhenia to the building that housed her apartment. Viktor opened the door for her again and escorted her to her door.

"Thank you," she replied, looking at Viktor. She was smiling again.

"No problem at all," Viktor replied. "Good night," he added as she opened the door and walked inside.

"Thank you. You too," Zhenia replied and closed the door behind her.

Viktor went outside and, for some reason, thought, *Does she really live alone? It's just scary to be alone in a new country.* Question after question poured into his head.

When he got back in the car, he immediately asked Henry, "Where did you meet Zhenia?"

He answered, "In our church. She was there with her mother and father."

"Okay, great. She lives with her mother and father. I thought she was alone," Viktor added.

"No, she lives with her parents. They all moved from Russia to Germany."

"Okay, you calmed me down. I was worried that she was the only one in such a serious condition."

"Yes, indeed, her situation is very serious, losing her husband and not knowing where he is and what is wrong with him," said Henry.

"Yes, and that too," replied Viktor.

Henry made a questioning expression on his face. "I don't understand you," he said.

Viktor replied, "I think she's pregnant. She didn't drink wine, and she has an appetite for two."

"What? You think she's pregnant?"

"Yes, I'm sure of it," Viktor replied. "Have you forgotten? I'm a psychologist."

"Do you think she knows she's pregnant?" asked Henry.

"Yes, I think she knows. She didn't drink alcoholic beverages."

Wow, Viktor thought. *How terrible it is to know that you will have a child and not know where your husband is. How terrible it is if her husband never knows that he will have or has a child. If he is alive.*

"This isn't Russia," he continued. "In Russia, in such cases, you can be removed without trial or investigation."

Henry said his thoughts aloud. "It's scary, terribly scary. Thank you, Grandpa Petro, for staying in Germany, for being born here."

"Yes, you're a lucky man," Viktor added.

"Excuse me, please," Henry said, suddenly realizing. "I didn't want to remind you of what happened to your parents."

"Henry," Viktor said, stopping him. "It is okay. No one knows what will happen to us or to our relatives or where or when. *C'est la vie.*"

They both fell silent, and then suddenly, Viktor said, "She is a pretty and very well-read girl. Do you know what she's finished and where she works?"

"She is a teacher at a foreign language school, German, English, and French. And she plays the piano," he added.

"Wow!" exclaimed Viktor. "And again, a girl who knows more than me—I mean foreign languages. My wife, Ella, taught me German and English."

Henry laughed. "Viktor, she's married, and they're going to have a baby. You're already making plans." He laughed loudly again.

"Henry," said Viktor, "I think that her husband died, and the child does not scare me. I personally dreamed of having a child with my wife. I think that God gave me a second wife, already with a child. I don't know why, but I think so. It's my destiny."

Viktor was silent for a moment. "I'm sorry. You probably think I'm crazy. I say such nonsense. It seems to me that this is exactly what happened. We'll see, but don't say a word to anyone, okay?"

"Of course. I will not say anything to anyone about this. But I think you would be a wonderful couple," he added.

Chapter 12
Fate

Two weeks passed. Viktor was invited to visit Patrick's home. He did not ask him anything, not even whether Zhenia and her parents would be at dinner, but for some reason, he wanted them to be there. He couldn't wait for Saturday. And finally, he, Martha, and Leo were on their way to dinner.

Martha knew nothing about the meeting of Viktor and Zhenia. It was the first time he had not said anything to his sister. He was afraid that she would call him frivolous.

Martha noticed that Viktor was dressed a little more elegantly than usual. He was trying to look attractive. She didn't ask, but she was glad that at last someone had made him do it. She hoped that it would be a new acquaintance at tonight's dinner.

Martha was looking forward to meeting her, and she watched him and said nothing to anyone. She was indescribably happy for Viktor, as his wife had died five years ago now.

When they arrived at Patrick's house, Viktor walked ahead of them, which never happened. He'd always been in the back all these years, wherever they went.

Martha nudged her husband in the side and whispered to him, "Do you know what's going on with him?"

"What's going on with him?" asked Leo. "Do you think something is wrong, something happened?"

"Quiet," said Martha. "I think he met someone. For some reason, he's keeping it a secret."

"Yes?" asked Leo in surprise. "It is okay. We'll all know when the time comes."

"Yes, of course. I'd just be very happy if he met anyone."

And then they saw Patrick and Henry standing on the doorstep, with a very pretty girl next to him.

Martha pushed her husband in the side again. "Look, I told you that Viktor's behavior must be related to a girl," she whispered.

Viktor immediately approached Zhenia. "Good afternoon," he said in Russian.

Martha was surprised. A thought flashed through her mind: *She's Russian.*

Viktor and Zhenia went inside the house together. Viktor was not interested in anything else happening around him. All his attention was paid only to Zhenia.

Henry walked up to Martha and said, "Good afternoon. Very nice to see you. We miss you. Yesterday, there was a conversation about you and your family all evening."

"What do you mean?" asked Martha.

"My dad and Zhenia's dad were talking about Zhenia's husband. Then about what happened to Zhenia."

"What happened to Zhenia? Is that, as I understand it, the girl who is in front with Viktor?" asked Martha.

"Yes." Henry told all the details to Martha and her husband.

With immense regret on her face, Martha said, "How horrible it is. How is it possible? I can imagine how she feels. Probably waiting every minute for a phone call with news of her missing husband."

Leo looked at Martha and thought, *He refused to volunteer and go to war with Ukraine. Everything is clear. He is no longer alive, and no one will ever find his body.* But he didn't want to say it out loud. It was clear to him; it happened very often in Russia. If you were a famous and popular person, you were first imprisoned and then destroyed. And if you were unknown to everyone, then this person simply disappeared, and no one knew what happened to him. It was scary. It had become normal, and everyone was afraid of the consequences. These times were reminiscent of the times of Stalin.

With these thoughts in mind, Leo went inside the house, where Patrick introduced him to Zhenia's father and mother. He said, "This is Ivan, and this is his wife, Olga. This is their daughter." He pointed to Zhenia. She was standing next to Viktor. "Her name is Zhenia. A very sad story, I'll tell you later."

"We know," Leo replied. "Henry has already told us what happened."

"Oh?" asked Patrick in surprise. "I pray for that young man, who is very strong in spirit, because he has his own opinion, which is very rare in Russia. Currently, all are intimidated by the new state laws."

They entered the room, and Patrick invited everyone to the table. Dinner was in a friendly—one might say family—atmosphere, like always. Patrick's family was joined by another new family from Russia. Zhenia's parents were also doctors, and they talked about the hospital and diseases. These were constant topics of conversation in Patrick's house. Martha was surprised by this since, after the death of his daughter, Patrick tried to avoid talking about the hospital. His face showed that he was having trouble talking until Martha changed the subject.

"Let's go to the hall," she suggested. "Zhenia said that she would love to play the piano for us."

Everyone clapped their hands. They gradually moved into the hall, and each of them found a comfortable place for themselves from which they could see and hear Zhenia play the piano.

Zhenia went to the piano, and she opened the lid and sat down on a chair. She very slowly put her hands on the keyboard, and for a few moments, she just sat there, staring somewhere in the distance, unknown to anyone.

No one could have imagined what she was thinking.

Zhenia thought that the last time she had played the piano was with her husband, Slava. She looked at her mother. Olga realized that Zhenia would not be able to play because she also remembered that day. It was a few days before he had disappeared.

Olga got up and went to Zhenia. She sat next to her and said, "Let's play together, you and me." She stroked her hand, and Zhenia smiled.

"Come on," Zhenia replied.

They began to play an excerpt from Tchaikovsky's work together, and it sounded very beautiful.

The musical moment in the room turned out to be very memorable for all those present. The music sounded like a heartfelt episode from the life of Zhenia. She played for her husband, Slava. In his absence unfortunately. Zhenia put all her feelings and thoughts into this musical fragment. She tried to express all her feelings for her husband, how much she missed him and how much she loved him.

After a while, Olga stopped playing with her daughter. She just sat next to her, tears rolling down her cheeks. She did not hide it. She just felt everything that was going on in her daughter's soul. She sobbed silently, and no one heard it.

But everyone saw how tears flowed down her cheeks and fell on her chest, and she did not wipe them. She just didn't want her daughter to see it. She sat motionless throughout the performance of the musical episode.

Zhenia finished playing, and she kept her hands on the keyboard again. She felt her husband's hands next to her. . . . Olga silently stroked her daughter's hand. She stood up and turned away. Only now did she wipe the tears from her face.

She turned to Zhenia again, put her arm around her shoulders, leaned over her, and said, "Zhenia, today's performance of this piece was just extraordinary."

"Really?" asked Zhenia, looking at everyone around her.

Everyone clapped their hands, and Viktor shouted, "Bravo, bravo, Zhenia."

Zhenia got up from the piano, smiled, bowed for everyone, and went out. She felt that she had to go outside; she did not have enough air. She almost ran out into the street as she walked along the path that led to the family cemetery, which she did not know about. She was just walking wherever this path led.

And then, she saw several monuments. She understood and immediately stopped. *Oh my gosh*, she thought. *Does Slava really want to tell me that he is dead?* She ran toward the standing monuments and began to read the names on them.

After reading every one, she calmed down. He was not in this place. She said out loud, "Fool. Of course he's not here. It's Patrick's family graveyard."

She sat down on a bench near the table, which stood next to a grave with the name Ella. *Oh my gosh. Ella. This is Viktor's wife. Viktor told me about it*, she thought.

She looked at the grave and thought, *How terrible it is to lose a loved one*. But then, she thought, *I don't know what is more terrible, knowing your husband is dead or not knowing what's wrong with him and where he is*.

She covered her face with her hands and started crying. She finally realized that she would probably never see her loved one again.

She sat there for a long time until, at last, Viktor found her. He had not expected to see her at his wife's grave.

He sat down next to her and said, "This is my wife, Ella. I miss her every day, even though it's been five years since she died."

Zhenia did not answer. He thought she probably wanted nothing at that moment, no one to see or talk to.

But suddenly, she turned to Viktor and said, "Viktor, I think that you and I met for a reason. You and I have both lost a person without whom we could not imagine our life."

Viktor told her, "Zhenia, you don't know about Slava yet. Maybe he's alive. Maybe one day you'll see him again. You have to believe. Miracles happen."

"I have to believe," she repeated. Zhenia looked at him. "I want to believe it, but something tells me that he died. I'm afraid it's true. I'll certainly believe it. But I have one very big trouble. No, this is not a problem; this is happiness," she corrected herself. "But I'm afraid that my child will grow up without a father. I'm pregnant," she said, turning to Viktor.

She looked at him and waited for an answer.

Viktor looked at her and replied, "I know; I'm a doctor. I knew it when we met at the restaurant. You've got a greatly increased appetite, and your face glows with happiness. And you didn't drink alcohol."

"Wow," replied Zhenia. "Not only are you a doctor, but you're like an investigator."

"Don't be upset," Viktor said. "I'll be with you all this time until your husband returns. Ella and I dreamed of having a large family, but unfortunately, we failed. I will be happy to be with your child until his father returns." He said it very seriously, looking her straight in the eyes.

Zhenia was amazed by his proposal. "Really?" she asked. "Will you do this, for me and my baby?"

"Yes," he replied very quickly.

Zhenia hugged him, and they sat hugging each other for a few seconds. Zhenia's head was spinning with indescribable gratitude to her friend. *My close friend*, she thought.

Chapter 13

A Baby Was Born

Zhenia and Viktor were inseparable. They announced to everyone that they were friends, that Viktor was helping her to deal with her very difficult situation, as he was a psychologist.

Of course, it was true, but on the part of Viktor, there were much more serious feelings toward Zhenia. He liked her, and he was very happy to spend all his free time with her. Since he no longer had his own apartment, he spent a lot of time with Zhenia in Martha and Leo's house or at Zhenia's house with her parents.

Zhenia was already eight months pregnant. She did not want to know the gender, but for some reason, she thought that it would be a girl. Zhenia's mother said that she would have a boy since the child lived very low in a pointed form. These were such female observations, a product of her many years.

Zhenia was ready for the birth of a child. Her parents transformed her room into a room for a child, with, of course, all the amenties Zhenia would need.

Early Saturday morning, the phone rang. Viktor had been waiting for this call. He had known that it would happen soon; the time had come for the birth of the child.

He immediately ran to the phone, and he heard Ivan's voice. "Good morning," Ivan said. "I'm going to take Zhenia to the hospital. She's in labor."

With great excitement in his voice, Viktor replied, "I'll be there very soon."

He ran out of the house and rushed to the hospital without telling Martha or Leo, as they were in their country house.

Arriving at the hospital, Viktor found the room where Zhenia was. She was already on the table for women in labor, and a midwife and a doctor were next to her. Viktor had to tell them that he was her husband so that he could be allowed into the room.

He immediately approached Zhenia. She took his hand and said, "Now I am ready to have a baby." She held Viktor's hand very tightly and cried in pain.

The doctor said, "Well done. Let's press on the abdomen. Push, push."

And again, the doctor advised Zhenia on what she needed to do: "Well done. Stop." she gave Zhenia advice almost every second.

"Okay, push."

Zhenia screamed again, and then, she heard the crying of her newborn.

"Congratulations," said the doctor. "You have a girl."

"A daughter," repeated Zhenia.

The doctor asked Viktor to cut the cord between the mother and the child. He looked at Zhenia with tears in his eyes and asked, "Do you want me to do this?"

"Yes," she replied.

The doctor looked at them and asked, "Why? Is he afraid to do this?"

"He's not afraid. It's the first time, and it's somehow unexpected," Zhenia replied.

She behaved very courageously, and Viktor was very excited and happy at the same time. *Cutting the cord between mother and child. How wonderful it is. This moment means that a new, almost independent person has been born,* Viktor thought. *Now she needs time and care from his mother, grandmother, grandfather, and, of course, father.*

But unfortunately, her father was absent, and it was unlikely that he would appear in the life of this girl. *It's a shame that he's not here, with his daughter, his wife,* Viktor thought. At such a very serious and responsible moment, he thought, *But it's okay that I will be her father if her mother doesn't mind because I love her.*

He caught himself on this word "love." He thought for a moment. He was absent now; he was not in the room. All his thoughts flew somewhere very far away. He regretted that Zhenia did not have her husband by her side now, and at the same time, he was glad that he was in his place.

But someone pulled his hand. It was Zhenia.

He woke up and looked over to her, and she was holding her daughter. The baby girl was lying on her chest and holding Zhenia by her finger. The baby girl's hand was so small, but she was already holding her mother's finger. The girl felt that, holding on to this finger, she was under the protection of her mother.

Zhenia's father took a photo of this unforgettable moment. Viktor came very close to Zhenia. He bent down and kissed the baby girl, and then, he kissed Zhenia on the lips. "Congratulations," he said.

She was surprised but at the same time very glad that he had done it. She knew and felt that Viktor was in love with her. Zhenia felt the same way, but since she was still married and still didn't know anything about her husband, she kept a distance in their relationship.

But now she had decided. *I don't want to be alone anymore,* she thought. *I want to be with him. He always makes me happy, no matter what happens, and no matter what he says, he takes care of me as his wife.*

The nurse said, "I'm sorry, but we need time to prepare for feeding the baby. I would ask everyone to leave, and it will be better if you all come tomorrow. She needs to sleep, and the child also needs to rest and gain strength."

Viktor and all those present approached Zhenia again.

"Congratulations again, Zhenia," he whispered in her ear. "I'm proud of you. You're a real loving mother." He kissed her on the lips again.

Ivan and Olga saw all this, but they said nothing. They were glad he had done it. They wanted their relationship to move from friendship to a more serious one since Viktor was next to her practically all the time, whenever he had a free minute.

When Viktor arrived home, he saw Martha's car. He entered the house and immediately saw her sitting at the table and making dumplings. Her husband loved them very much, and she cooked for him very often.

"Good afternoon," said Martha. "Where have you been? I arrived very early in the morning, and you were no longer at home."

"Zhenia gave birth to a girl," Viktor replied briefly. He sank down beside Martha in a chair by the table.

"A girl!" said Martha with delight.

"I've just come from the hospital. I'll go again tomorrow morning. The doctors advised so."

"I'll go with you," Martha replied. "How is she?"

"She handled herself perfectly. It was very scary for me," he added. "I was worried. I cut the cord, and for some reason, it scared me very much."

"Why?" asked Martha in surprise. "You're allowed to do that. They know you're just friends."

"I deceived them. I said that I was her husband," Viktor replied.

Martha looked at him and said nothing. She was waiting for a more serious description of this act. And she was right to do so.

After a second, Viktor looked at her and said, "Martha, you know I love her." He fell silent again. "I don't know what to do. But I'm sure I want to be with them. I think I should propose to her."

Martha did not answer. She looked at her brother and did not know what to advise him.

Viktor asked, "Why are you silent?"

The words got stuck in her throat. She really didn't know what to advise him, and she asked him, "Did you ask Zhenia what she thought about this?"

"No, I haven't spoken to her, but I'll talk to her tomorrow when we're alone."

"Okay, I won't disturb you. I'll go later."

"No, I want us to go together, and then you can leave. I want her to know that we really care about her as a member of our family." Then, he asked, "When will Leo be home?"

He heard the front door open, and Leo walked in. He immediately joined the conversation: "Good evening. I see everyone's at home and my dumplings are ready. I'm starving to death. I've got three days off this weekend. I want to go out of town." He didn't stop talking about his plans.

He fell silent when Martha and Viktor looked at him and did not answer. "What happened?" Leo asked.

"Everything's okay," Martha replied. "Just this morning, Zhenia gave birth to a baby girl, and Viktor has just returned from the hospital."

"That's great news!" exclaimed Leo.

"Yes, this is very good news, but I want to talk to you," Viktor said.

"Of course," Leo replied. "But first, I'll go take a shower."

"And I," said Martha, "I'll go cook the dumplings, and we'll have lunch and discuss everything at the table, okay?"

"Of course," Viktor agreed. He also went to his room and took a quick, refreshing shower.

When Viktor left his room, the table was already set, and Martha and Leo were seated. Martha poured him a plate of freshly cooked borscht. Viktor was very excited, and he was always hungry.

They ate in silence.

After he ate his soup, he asked, "I'd like to talk to you about Zhenia. I want to propose to her, and if she agrees to marry me, I'd like to bring her here. She lives with her parents, and they have only two rooms. She will have to sleep on the sofa in the living room because her room will become the baby's room. She would do anything for her child."

Leo immediately chimed in, "Viktor, listen to me carefully. Even if she doesn't give you an agreement, you should still offer to let her move here. It will be close to her parents, and her mother will be able to help her with the child. I know she's going to need help the first few months."

"Really?" asked Viktor.

"Yes," Leo replied. "We all know you've loved her for a very long time, and maybe living together will bring your relationship closer. The house is big. There is enough space for everyone. It will be convenient for you. Her mom can live here if she wants, and her father can too so that they are all together to support Zhenia."

Viktor was very happy and beamed with joy. He said, "Martha, do you remember what I told you when we were driving from Mariupol to Lviv? That Leo has a huge heart. He helps everyone."

"Yes, I remember you scared me then. I thought you were exaggerating. But I became convinced of this very quickly. We need to organize a room for the child."

"Girl. Did you give her a name?" Leo asked.

"I think I'm going to let Zhenia make that decision."

"Of course," Leo said. "Tomorrow morning, we will all go to the hospital and discuss all this. I will offer to let her move to our house, and you will propose to her, here in our house. She will be ready to accept your offer."

"OMG," Martha said. "You're absolutely right. Great idea."

"Thank you. Thank you very much," Viktor replied.

Chapter 14
New Home

The next day, Martha cooked breakfast, and they once again discussed how they would offer their house to Zhenia. After discussing all the details, they went to the hospital.

Zhenia was busy. She was feeding the baby, and they were told that they had to wait five to ten minutes. They sat down in the corridor near the room, and then, they saw that Zhenia's parents were walking down the corridor in their direction.

Leo got up and walked toward them. "Good morning," he said. "Everyone woke up early today, but we all have to wait for Zhenia to be available. The nurse warned us that she was feeding the little girl. We don't know her name yet."

The nurse then invited everyone into the ward, and they followed the others.

Viktor did not yet know that Zhenia had named the girl Ella in honor of his wife.

Entering the room, Viktor immediately approached Zhenia. The baby girl was lying next to her in the crib. After eating, she had already fallen asleep.

"Good morning," Viktor said.

"Good morning," Zhenia replied. "I have news." She turned to Viktor. "Do you remember when we were sitting at your wife's grave? I said that, if I had a girl, I would name her after your wife, Ella, and if I had a boy, I would name him after my husband, Slava."

"Of course I remember that," Viktor replied.

"So, I gave my daughter the name Ella." She looked at Viktor and waited for his approval.

But he looked at Zhenia and said nothing. Many questions were spinning in his head. He was not sure it was right that the baby was named after his wife. He didn't know what to say, and he didn't know that it would be comfortable in their position to name the girl after Ella. Because he was going to propose to Zhenia.

Viktor did not want to upset Zhenia, so smiling lightly, he said, "Okay. Ella. Let it be Ella."

Martha saw his expression; she knew her brother. She realized that he did not agree with this, but he was a very nice person and did not want to offend Zhenia. Martha thought, *Okay, they will have more time on this topic after everyone leaves.*

Everyone very quietly approached the crib in which the girl was lying. They admired her. She looked like Zhenia, with dark hair and chubby cheeks, and when she smiled, a dimple appeared on one of her cheeks. This gave her some kind of special charm. She was sleeping and moving her hands, and suddenly, she sneezed.

Everyone said in unison, "Be healthy," and it was a moment that gave special attention to the girl.

"She sneezed," everyone repeated, as if it had never happened, as if something very special had happened, like everyone was happy with everything she did. "She sneezed," "She moved her right hand," "She moved her leg," "She has a dimple on her cheek," and so on. . . .

It was the indescribable pleasure of having a newborn. Everyone was in awe of everything she did, and it would be a long time until she could walk and talk. When a new person is born with new habits, with a new name, the human pleasure in everything that happens to them lasts for a very long time.

One by one, everyone began to disperse. Zhenia's parents were the first to leave, so Martha and Leo and Viktor were left alone with Zhenia.

Leo said, "Zhenia, I want to talk to you about your place of residence. I found out that your parents only have two rooms and that you will sleep on the couch in the living room. I don't think it's convenient for a young mother."

Everyone looked at Zhenia.

She replied, "This does not scare me. I want my baby girl Ella to be calm and don't want anything to bother her, so I decided to convert my room into a room for a child. I don't care where I sleep."

"I understand you," Leo said. "We make all kinds of conveniences for our children, regardless of our inconveniences. But this need not be the case. We thought about it and decided to make you an offer to move into our house.

"We have so many rooms in the house, and there are only three of us. We discussed this matter and decided that the entire first floor belongs to you. One room for you, the other for Ella, one for Viktor, and in the fourth room, your mother and father can move in, as you will need your mother's help.

I think God gave us our four rooms for some reason. Now we have found out for what reason He gave them. He was thinking about you and your child. You need all the necessary conditions, as I know how difficult it is to have your first child and not have all the comforts. I think it's just a great idea.

"Me and Martha, very often, we live outside the city. You will practically all live together in our home. Personally, I like it," Leo continued. "There will be many people living in the house again, and everyone will be comfortable. Even those living in the house now will feel very comfortable with everyone living in it."

Zhenia looked at Martha and Leo, and all this time, she had not said one word.

"Well, do you agree?" Martha asked.

Zhenia covered her face with her hands, stuck her head into the pillow, and cried.

Everyone looked at each other.

Viktor said in a whisper, "I hope we didn't offend you with our proposal."

Zhenia raised her head and said, "Offended? What are you talking about? You are all my closest friends, and I am just amazed by your proposal."

Viktor breathed a deep sigh of relief.

"I was scared," Leo said. "Why are you crying? That we offended you came to my mind."

Zhenia replied, "Thank you very much. I don't know how to thank you. I don't know how many times I have already said 'Thank you very much.' Thank you very much for your good nature and generosity."

"Just let me play with Ella sometimes," Viktor said. "I would be very happy with this gift."

"Of course! I'll be happy if you want to spend time with her. I think she'll love you more than she loves me."

"Well, that's too much. Children always love their mother more than their father," Viktor said.

"No, you're wrong. Girls love their father more; that's why they are called daddy's girls."

At that moment, a thought flashed through Viktor's head: *This child does not have a father. It's a pity that we are talking about this topic.* He tried to change the subject. "Don't worry," he said. "We will move everything and organize a room for Ella and for you."

"Thank you very much," Zhenia replied again. "I'll probably start counting how many times I say 'Thank you so much,'" she joked. The tears, which were tears of joy, did not dry in her eyes, and they rolled down her cheeks.

Martha said, "We only have two days to take care of your move." So, she and Leo said goodbye and left.

Viktor remained alone with Zhenia, and they both admired Ella. He said, "I'll go too. I need to help Martha and Leo." He leaned over to Zhenia again, and he kissed her on the lips, this time for longer.

Zhenia was not surprised; she was happy with this kiss. Viktor was glad that she didn't resist and didn't say anything, as if it was normal between them.

Viktor returned home, and all three of them began to move the furniture, creating convenience for the newborn and for Zhenia.

Zhenia called her parents and told them the news. Her mother was glad that she could be with Zhenia and help her. They transported Zhenia's things and everything necessary for the baby's room.

The child's room turned out to be spacious, bright, and comfortable. Between the child's room and the room where she would live, Zhenia had doors. She could enter her daughter's room anytime. It was a very convenient location for a newborn baby and a young mother.

Chapter 15
Hope for the Future

After two days, the whole family gathered at Leo and Martha's house, waiting for the return of Viktor and the arrival of Zhenia and her child at their new home, which foretold a happy future for both of them.

Viktor went to the hospital for Zhenia and her daughter. He was in high spirits. In the back seat of his car, there were two huge bouquets of flowers. He had decided to give one to the attending physician and, of course, one to Zhenia.

He took the flowers and went inside the building. First, he found the attending physician and handed her the first bouquet, thanking her for everything at the same time. Then, he went to the ward where Zhenia was. When he opened the door, he saw Zhenia standing near the window and holding her daughter in her arms.

When she saw Viktor, she beamed with joy and happiness. "I saw you when you parked your car. We've been waiting for you all morning," Zhenia said.

"I'm sorry. I didn't know you would be discharged so early," Viktor replied.

"Don't worry. It's okay. I've spent the whole morning with Ella. We studied each other. I could not imagine that, at such an age, she could already look at me like a student. I think it only looks like that. She does not perceive everything that is happening yet, but she clearly looks at me and smiles," Zhenia said.

Viktor was looking at Zhenia and listening to her without interrupting when she stopped, or rather, took a break in her story. Viktor took advantage of this moment and said, "Honey, this is for you."

He handed her the second bouquet of flowers, consisting of twenty tea roses. Their smell spread a long distance. Viktor knew that these were her favorite flowers. They grew on the estate of her house in Russia. She had told him that her mom had planted these flowers for her when she was born. Since then, this bush had grown into many bushes that surrounded one side of their house. Zhenia very often remembered them. Viktor even thought that he should plant such a bush for Ella after Zhenia moved into his house.

Zhenia put Ella on the bed, took the bouquet of flowers, and sniffed them, and tears appeared in her eyes. She looked at Viktor and asked, "Do you remember that these are my favorite flowers?"

"Yes, I remember," he replied. "And I agree with you; they are simply unique in beauty and smell. They cannot be compared with anything. You have excellent taste."

Zhenia came up to Viktor and hugged and kissed him, but as a friend.

Viktor thought, *It is okay. She needs time to decide. I'm patient. I'll wait.*

* * *

Zhenia had been living in Leo and Martha's house for eleven months, and the girl had grown up. For the first three months, Zhenia's mother had lived with her and only went home for the weekend. But now she was at home with her husband all week and came only on weekends to admire her granddaughter.

Viktor spent all his free time with Ella. He was glad that everything had turned out this way for them. Ella slept from nine o'clock in the evening to nine o'clock in the morning without any problems. Zhenia had enough time to sleep, and she felt great. She didn't feel tired, and she had enough time for everything. She was organized. She made a routine for herself and strictly followed it.

Viktor usually fed Ella in the morning and then left for the university. When he returned in the evening, he fed her again and put her to bed. Ella was used to seeing him every morning, and she saw him in the evening before she went to bed.

One fine day, when Viktor was getting up in the morning to feed her, she suddenly said, "Pa."

Viktor was stunned. *Her first word. Dad*, he thought. He immediately shouted to Zhenia, "Zhenia, come here!"

Zhenia was in the kitchen, and she did not hear him. Viktor changed Ella's diaper, took her in his arms, and then went to the kitchen.

As soon as he entered the kitchen, he said, "Zhenia! Ella said her first word. She said, 'Pa.'"

"I know. I taught her. I told her almost every day, 'Papa,' and finally, she said 'Pa' yesterday for the first time."

Viktor asked, "Why did you teach her to say Dad? You need to teach her to say Mom."

"And now I'm going to teach her to say Mom," Zhenia answered. She did not answer why she had taught Ella to say the word "Papa."

They were very glad that Ella had begun to speak. After Dad, she very quickly learned to say Mom. Then, she said "Mar," which meant Martha. And she knew the dog said "Woof, woof."

Then, life for Ella began to turn into the study of the Russian language.

And then, her first birthday came. Absolutely all friends and relatives were invited—all of Patrick's family, Pawel's family, and all their children. Martha and Leo's house was filled.

Martha organized a festive dinner for Ella. She received many gifts and, of course, a huge cake.

All the relatives and friends took photos one by one. She was used to them; they visited her very often. But still she stretched out her hands in the direction of Viktor. Everyone noticed that she loved him as a father, but they didn't say anything. Everyone knew that he was going to propose to Zhenia, but when exactly this would happen, no one knew, and of course, he would not propose on the birthday of her daughter.

In the evening, when everyone had dispersed, it was put in order. Viktor took up his duties. He fed Ella, and then, after reading a few books to her, he put her to bed.

As soon as he closed the door behind him, Zhenia was waiting for him. She took him by the hand and pulled him to her room. Viktor did not understand what was happening, but he did not resist.

Once he entered Zhenia's room, she closed the doors behind him. She hugged him and said, "Thank you for everything you and your family have done for us. All this time, I knew that I had feelings for you. I love you."

Viktor looked at her and, without saying a word, began to kiss her. He kissed her for a long time on her lips and on her eyelids, and after that, he said, "I love you. I fell in love with you back then in the restaurant when we first met."

Zhenia replied, "I know. I saw it, but I wasn't sure how I felt. I still hoped for my husband's return. But now I know for sure that this was a vain wait. And now I know that I love you."

They sat in the room for a long time, talking about their feelings and understanding of the situation.

Then, Viktor said, "I'm hungry. For some reason, I didn't eat when we had guests."

Zhenia answered, "Let's go to the kitchen. I'll cook you anything." She laughed. "I don't want to have a hungry fiancé."

Viktor stopped her. "What? What did you say? Did you call me a fiancé?"

"Yes," replied Zhenia. "I want to be your bride. Unless, of course, you have another?"

Viktor laughed. "I don't have anyone but you." And he began to kiss her again.

Zhenia pulled him to the kitchen. She prepared dumplings for him. She fried them in oil. It reminded him of his house and his mother. She also reminded him of home when she wanted to warm them up. He told Zhenia about it, and of course, she remembered it and had decided to remind him of it tonight. She didn't say anything; she just did the same things his mom did.

Chapter 16

Happiness and Grief

Viktor could not wait to see his sister and tell her the news the next morning. Zhenia had proposed to him, but he did not tell anyone about it. He would propose to his girlfriend.

He woke up very early, as always, and he fed his future daughter and went to the institute. He decided that he would stop by the hospital since he knew that Martha was working today.

He drove up to the hospital and saw Martha just parking her car. He stopped next to her, opened the window, and said, "Good morning, sister." There was a note of mystery in his voice.

"Good morning. What are you doing here?" she asked, stepping up to his car and talking through the open window.

"I have some amazing news."

"Really?" asked Martha. "Don't answer. I know you proposed to Zhenia."

"No, I didn't. Zhenia proposed to me," he replied. "She said—and I'll tell you word for word—she said she would like to be my fiancé."

"Oh my gosh. It's just a miracle. I'm happy for you," replied Martha. "And what are you going to do now?"

"I'll propose to her, but I don't know where and when."

"And what are you going to do with the ring?" she asked.

"Yes, this is also a big problem. I don't want to give her my wife's ring. But this ring belongs to our mother," he thought aloud.

"Viktor, I think that I will take this ring for myself since I got this ring from our mother. I will keep it as a memory of our mother and, of course, Ella. I'll help you buy a new ring for Zhenia."

"Thank you, thank you," Viktor replied. "I'll pay you back as soon as I start working, and this will happen very soon. I'm so glad I'm graduating this year. As I planned with Ella, I am opening my own clinic—but only one—and maybe then I will start recruiting a group of psychotherapists."

"Yes, I agree with you. I think you will succeed. You are a very successful doctor, and the clinic will give you more opportunities for prosperity and responsibility. Just come up with something very memorable for the proposal," Martha added.

"Yes, I'm trying. But nothing comes to my mind."

"Let's go buy a ring tomorrow and talk about it," Martha suggested.

"Okay," Viktor replied.

"I have to leave. I'm having a very busy day; a lot of wounded were brought in yesterday. From Ukraine," Martha said.

"Bye," Viktor replied. He blew her kisses and drove to the university.

Having gone to work, Martha began, as always, to look through all the documents for the new patients who were being prepared for operation today. She opened folder after folder.

The last folder seemed very surprising to her. The patient had no name, no surname, and no address. He was unconscious. *This is the case*, she thought. She got up from the table and went to the room where he was lying. Entering the room, she went to the bed. He was a young, very handsome man, about twenty or thirty years old.

He had a very tanned body and a burned nose and cheeks, as if he had been on the street without cover from the sun.

I need Viktor and his logical professional thinking as a psychologist, she thought.

The patient had long hair, as if he had not cut it for a long time, and a long beard, which meant that he had not have the opportunity to shave.

So he's not a soldier, Martha thought. *Who is this man?* She was worried about this matter. And then she thought about her grandfather Petro. He had also been found wounded. Berta had found him, and to save him, she had changed his Russian soldier clothes to German clothes, which she had taken from the dead soldier lying next to him.

Martha remembered how Berta had said, "I am a nurse, and I must help the wounded regardless of their nationality." Martha thought, *No matter what, we must save this young man.*

She ordered him to be shaved, trimmed, and washed before the operation. She wrote down all these orders on the patient's card.

The woman who changed his clothes checked all his pockets, hoping to find information about him. But she did not find a single document—only a small photo of a young girl. *It's his wife or fiancé*, the woman thought.

After all the procedures, they cut his hair, shaved him, washed him, and dressed him in all new pajamas to be hospitalized. The nurse put all his belongings neatly in a plastic bag, and she held the photo in her hands. She thought of putting the picture inside with her things or maybe giving it to the other nurse. She thought, *Where are all his other documents so that this photo is not lost, as it's very important for this young man?*

She went to the operating room and found Martha and said, "These are all the belongings of that young man who is unconscious without documents."

Martha replied, "Put them in his room. We have to wash his clothes so that he can change into them after he recovers."

"Okay," she agreed. "I'll take care of it." She was still standing near Martha.

"What else?" asked Martha.

"I found this photo in his pocket. I don't know where to put it. Should it go with his belongings, or should I give it to you?" she asked.

"Photo?" asked Martha.

"Yes," replied Hena–that was the woman's name. "I'll take this and put it with his documents. It's still some kind of document. Maybe we can find this girl and find out who this stranger is."

Martha reached out to take the photo from Hena. "Thank you," she said.

Taking the photo in her hands, she looked over it. Martha immediately had a very concerned and excited face. She stared at the photo and said nothing. She was amazed at what she saw. It was a photo of Zhenia.

This young man is Zhenia's husband, Martha thought. "OMG," she said.

"What's wrong?" asked Hena.

"I know this girl. Her name is Zhenia. This young man is her husband. She lost him two years ago," replied Martha.

"Wow, what luck. We found her husband. She will be very happy. I am happy to see them be back together again after a long separation," added Hena.

"Yes. . . ." Martha said. *I don't know that Zhenia will be happy to see him after two years of separation. Or maybe she is still waiting for him,* she thought. She doubted this very much since she knew of the relationship between Zhenia and her brother. But at that moment, a thought slipped through her head: *I am not sure that this will bring happiness to my brother. Zhenia also fell in love with Viktor, and her daughter has called him Daddy.* All this sounded in her head like a sentence in court.

What should I do? she thought. *I cannot tell Zhenia. I must tell the attending physician and the surgeon about it. Let them decide since I cannot make this decision. I am only a nurse.*

She calmed herself down, immediately took all his documents, and went to the surgeon first. She told him everything she had learned about the new patient.

The surgeon was her husband, Leo. Leo looked at the photo of Zhenia, and he said, "This find . . . you would never have thought that this could happen. Calm down. Don't worry. Everything will be fine. Zhenia has found her husband, and that's great."

Martha almost screamed, "Leo, what are you talking about? Zhenia proposed to Viktor last night. Her daughter calls Viktor 'Daddy.' He has been in love with Zhenia for more than two years. How can you say that it is okay that Zhenia has found her husband?"

Martha looked at Leo, and he fell silent and looked back at her.

"Oh my gosh," he said suddenly. "I didn't know that Zhenia proposed to Viktor. I thought that she was waiting for her husband. They tell everyone they're just friends." Then, he looked at Martha and said, "I can't operate on him. We have to find the attending physician and tell him everything."

After explaining the situation, Leo said to the attending physician, "I can't operate on him; you have to replace me."

"Of course," the attending physician agreed. "This is against the law otherwise."

Martha watched Zhenia's husband all day after the operation. When the patient was brought back to his room, she went to talk to his surgeon. "Well, how is his condition?" she asked.

The surgeon replied, "We did everything we could. Let's hope that his young body wins out over all his problems. He is still unconscious now."

Martha asked, "What should I do with Zhenia? Should I tell her that we have found her husband, or will we wait for him to wake up?"

"We are obliged to inform his wife," the surgeon replied.

"All right," replied Martha. "I'll tell her tonight. It's a special case. I don't want to talk to her on the phone about this topic. I must make sure she's safe. Tomorrow morning, I will bring her to the hospital, and we will tell her everything."

"It's late today, and he needs rest after the surgery," the surgeon added. "Tomorrow morning will be the best time to meet and talk."

"See you tomorrow," said Martha.

She was walking along the corridor toward her office when she saw her brother coming toward her. She was amazed at this because she did not want to talk to Viktor about this topic now. "What are you doing here?" she asked.

A happy smile shone on Viktor's face.

Martha said, "Let's go to the office. We need to talk."

Viktor was surprised that she would invite him into the office. Usually, they talked surrounded by her employees and colleagues.

After they entered the office, she closed the doors. She had a folder with the documents belonging to Zhenia's husband, including the photo of Zhenia.

Martha sat Viktor on a sofa that stood near the wall. This office was always used in very serious cases, when they informed relatives about a death or decided to turn off the device that kept a patient alive. She sat down next to Viktor.

He looked at Martha, and then he realized that something had happened. "Martha, what happened? Hurry and tell me the truth. I am a very strong-willed person. I do not like all these long conversations. I know. I will do this with my clients too, but I am a doctor, and I know that something has happened. What's wrong?" Viktor asked.

Martha took the photo out of the folder and gave it to Viktor.

He took it, examined it, and asked, "This is Zhenia, right?"

"Yes," replied Martha.

"Where did you get this photo?" asked Viktor.

"In the pocket of her husband's jacket," replied Martha.

Viktor looked at her for a few seconds. "What?" he asked. "Do you mean that you have found Zhenia's husband?"

"Yes," replied Martha.

"Is he here in the hospital?"

"Yes," replied Martha again.

Viktor looked at the photo. "She's very young here. They've known each other for years," he said.

"Yes," said Martha.

She was amazed at how her brother was controlling himself, but at the same time, she was afraid that he would explode and get a broken heart.

She immediately got up from the sofa and, without asking him, gave him a sedative. He did not resist; he knew that he needed it. Sometimes, it's good to be a doctor—you don't have to ask additional questions.

After taking the medicine, he asked, "Can I see him first, before Zhenia?"

"Yes, it is possible," replied Martha. But then she thought about it and said, "Viktor, do you think that's a good idea? Maybe it's better if you don't see him."

"No," he replied. "I want to see him."

"Viktor, he is currently unconscious after surgery," said Martha. "And the surgeon said it would be better if we brought Zhenia tomorrow morning. Maybe he'll be awake by then."

"Please," Viktor begged.

"No, it's not really allowed," Martha said. "If anything happens to him, you'll be under suspicion. I can't show him to you until tomorrow. First Zhenia, and then you, if she invites you. You can't see him without anyone because you're in a relationship with his wife. I'm sorry. Let's go home. We'll leave your car here in the parking lot, as you can't drive after taking medication."

Viktor got up from the sofa. "Let's go," he said in a very depressed voice.

Martha took his arm, and they went to the parking lot. Viktor was silent all the way home.

Entering the house, he was met by Zhenia. She was holding her daughter in her arms.

"Daddy," Ella shouted and stretched out her hands to him.

Tears flowed down Viktor's cheeks. He walked up to them, hugged them both, and said, "I have to go to my room. I'm sorry." He kissed Ella and walked in the direction of his room.

Zhenia looked at Martha. "What's wrong? I have not seen him in this condition ever. What did he drink with his friends?" she asked.

"Nothing," replied Martha. "Let's go to the hall. I have to talk to you. Where's Leo?"

"He's in the kitchen, cooking something for dinner," Zhenia replied.

"Okay then, let's go to the kitchen," Martha replied.

Going into the kitchen, Martha saw that her husband had set the table. He had set it up for four. He did not know that Viktor would not be able to participate in this very important conversation.

"The table is ready for our dinner and serious conversation," Leo said. "Welcome." He seated Zhenia and set up a chair for Ella. Martha and Leo looked at Zhenia.

Martha said, "I think I'm going to start our conversation."

Leo nodded in agreement.

"What's wrong?" asked Zhenia. "You're both acting strange."

"Yes," Leo replied. "We have a very good reason for that."

Martha took out Zhenia's photo from the folder and handed it to Zhenia. Zhenia took the photo, and at that moment, she realized that they had found her husband.

"Is he here?" asked Zhenia with tears in her eyes. "Where is he?"

Leo replied, "He's in the hospital, but he's still unconscious. He underwent surgery today, as he was found wounded. They took him to the hospital, but he was undocumented and unconscious. Just today, one of the nurses found this photo in his jacket. She brought this photo to Martha, and then we realized who he was. But we still did not know his full name."

Zhenia told them his full name, and Martha wrote it down in the folder.

"Year of birth and date?" asked Martha.

Zhenia answered again, and Martha wrote it down.

"Place of birth."

Zhenia answered again. Martha wrote it down, and on it went for several minutes.

"I knew that this would happen at the very moment when I decided to become Viktor's wife," Zhenia said. "It happened. He disappeared, leaving me alone, pregnant. My daughter has a dad, she loves Viktor, and I love him. I can't be his wife. As soon as he recovers, I will file for divorce. Is it possible? Yes?" she asked.

"I don't know exactly," Leo replied. "But you got married in Russia. There are probably some special rules for that."

"How? How did he end up in Ukraine? How long has he been hiding? More than two years?" Martha reasoned aloud.

"But I want to be honest," Zhenia said. "I don't want to see him. I don't know why, but I didn't expect him anymore. All my pain and love and pity for him disappeared during these two years. I have never seen such a selfless, loving person as Viktor. He was there for me all these years. He loved me without reciprocation.

"I am glad that I met him, and I am not afraid to explain all this to my husband. He is my husband on paper but not in my heart. I don't love him anymore. I love Viktor, and my daughter has a father. She loves him. I can't deprive her of her father, with whom she spent nine months in my belly and more than a year in real life. Viktor has been taking care of us for more than two years.

"Martha, I love him," said Zhenia, looking at Martha.

Suddenly, she began to cry. "Would Slava not understand this? Because it's not fair. I don't know what will happen to him. But I know what will happen to me and my daughter. I only want to be with Viktor."

Leo joined the conversation: "Zhenia, let's talk about everything tomorrow. I'm hungry. I'm glad you and Viktor will be together, and we'll help you."

Zhenia smiled. "Thank you. I'm hungry too. I'm always hungry when I'm worried."

They began to have dinner, and everyone realized that their worries were in vain. More than two years had passed since the disappearance of Zhenia's husband, and life had changed its course, as had happened to Martha's Grandpa Petro.

War changes the lives of many people, regardless of circumstance.

Chapter 17
Hello and Goodbye

The next morning, Zhenia, with her parents and her daughter in tow, went to the hospital to meet her husband after two years of separation.

Martha and Leo were already at work. First, they went to the ward to find out about the patient's state of health, but he was not there.

"Where is he?" asked Martha, looking at Leo.

"I don't know," he replied in confusion.

They went to the attending physician's office.

As soon as they entered his office, he replied, "I'm sorry, but we did everything we could. His heart just couldn't take it. He was very exhausted, and his body was in critical condition."

Martha was very upset that he would not meet his daughter. "What a pity that he was so close to his daughter and could not see her, could not get to know her," she said.

When Zhenia and her parents arrived, Leo explained to them everything that had happened: "He was found unconscious, and after the operation, he never regained consciousness. His body was very emaciated. He went through great obstacles to get to Ukraine. We will never know the full truth of what happened to him." He apologized again.

"Can we see him?" Zhenia's father asked.

"Yes, you must see him, and not only see him, but you must also identify him since he has no documents, only a photo of your daughter, Zhenia."

Leo and Martha led them to the morgue. Martha asked Viktor to stay with Ella in the office since Zhenia did not want her daughter to see her father dead. "She didn't see him alive either, so why should she see him dead?" she had said. "She is still too small to realize what is happening. I don't want her to be in the morgue with me."

Everyone agreed with her.

Viktor agreed with her. Even he had lost the desire to see Zhenia's husband. *Why do I need this? I don't know him, and I don't want to see him. I know that Zhenia was married, but this is the past, and it does not concern me in any way. I want to live with Zhenia in the future, a happy future*, he thought.

He took Ella in his arms, and they began to read the book she loved. There were many animals in it, and she always made all their sounds–the dog's "Woof, woof," the cat's "Meow," the rabbit's "Hop, hop, hop." Ella repeated all of them. The father and daughter read the book and were happy no matter what, and they didn't want to know what was in the past.

Zhenia and her parents entered the morgue, and Leo asked, "Are you all ready?"

"Yes," replied Zhenia. Her heart was pounding at a tremendous speed.

A thought flashed through her head: *Maybe it isn't him; maybe it's just an accident. Maybe he gave my picture to someone. Wow,* she thought. *Am I still hoping that he will return?*

The doctor opened the door of the refrigerator where the body lay.

Zhenia recognized him at once. "Yes, this is my husband," she said. She looked at him and said, "Hello, Slava. It's a pity that it happened this way. I offer my deep regrets for the torment you have endured during these two years."

She continued, "I have a daughter. Her name is Ella. I think you'd be happy to see her, but I understand it's not fate. We will bury you in the family cemetery, and we will come to see you. Of course, I will tell Ella about you but not now. Only when she can understand what happened." Zhenia put her hand on his head and said, "Hello and goodbye."

And she got out of the morgue. Martha followed her. Her parents lingered for a moment. They probably also said hello and goodbye to their son-in-law.

This is life. We say hello when we meet and say goodbye when we part forever, Zhenia thought.

The war had forced this young couple to break up and meet again, but unfortunately, nothing could be changed.

That was why Zhenia had to say, "Hello, Slava."

I've been waiting for you for so long, and now I have no way out. I can only say goodbye to you. We have a daughter. Thank you for this amazing gift. I hope that you will see her and protect her throughout her life. Zhenia said those words to herself. No one heard them except her husband in the sky.

Every ending brings the promise of a new beginning.

About the Author

August 17, 1995, is the happiest day of Linda Hope's life. It was the day her family landed at Miami International Airport. From that day on, she and her family celebrated August 17 like it was a family birthday.

Linda was born in Siberia in 1956. At the age of six, on September 1, 1962, she was sent to an orphanage. Until the sixth grade, she studied in the orphanage.

In 1970, she moved to the Caucasus with her grandmother Polina. Then, in 1972, she graduated from high school. Finally having freedom, she left and moved as far from her family as possible.

She graduated from a trade school in the city of Engels, which is in the Saratov region. After that, she attended a polytechnic institute and eventually graduated.

In 1975, she got married. Three years later, in 1978, she gave birth to a son. Then, in 1984, she had a daughter.

Six years later, she opened the first private enterprise in her city. But then she started having issues with her husband, who was a great communist. For four years, she fought to keep her family together, but at the same time, she learned to accept the situation.

In 1994, she was forced to make a life-changing decision— to leave her husband. Her political views in no way coincided with the political views of Russia. So, in 1995, she made the journey to America.

www.ingramcontent.com/pod-product-compliance
Lightning Source LLC
LaVergne TN
LVHW011834060526
838200LV00053B/4011